SCIENCE FICTION HANDBOOK, *REVISED*

A Guide to Writing Imaginative Literature

SCIENCE FICTION HANDBOOK, *REVISED*

L. Sprague de Camp

and

Catherine Crook de Camp

1975

Owlswick Press   Philadelphia

To George H. Scithers

without whose consummate skill at slave-driving, this book would never have gone to press when it did.

CONTENTS

Half title and title page illustrations: Don Simpson

Typesetting by LUNA Publications

Photography by Advanced Litho and
Cage Graphic Arts

Printing and Binding by R. R. Donnelley & Sons

PREFACE

L. Sprague de Camp's original *Science-Fiction Handbook,* published in 1953 and long out of print, has been favorably remembered by a whole generation of science-fiction readers and aspiring writers. Over the years, at convention after convention, fans have urged its reissue. Teachers of courses on imaginative fiction have begged for the book; one planned to reproduce the manual for his creative writing course until he learned that the material was under copyright. Because of this enduring interest, the present book came into being.

The original handbook has been entirely rewritten. Obsolete passages have been deleted. The history of science fiction and fantasy has been updated. Chapters have been added to give apprentice writers information about the legal, financial, and housekeeping aspects of the writing profession. The book includes a number of important lessons learned the hard way by the de Camps in the course of their long writing career.

Genius may be a gift from the gods, but competence in the craft of writing must be acquired. The skills of writing professionally can be learned by anyone who takes the time to do so. Even the most talented person must know how to protect, peddle, and promote his literary works. For those who want to learn both skills, this book has been designed.

The original *Science-Fiction Handbook* was made possible by the generous coöperation of many friends, acquaintances, and colleagues—several of whom have now, alas, joined the majority. For answering questions, granting permission to quote from letters and other writings, offering useful advice, and—in some cases—criticizing parts of the manuscript, we are grateful to Forrest J Ackerman, Harry Altshuler, Isaac Asimov, Everett F. Bleiler, Anthony Boucher, Leigh Brackett, Ray Bradbury, Walter I. Bradbury, Howard Browne, John W. Campbell, Thomas Clareson, Inga Pratt Clark, John D. Clark, Sol Cohen, Alan C. Collins, Lester del Rey, August W. Derleth, Lord Dunsany, Lloyd Arthur Eshbach, Dennis Flanagan, Oscar J. Friend, Mary Gnaedinger, Horace L. Gold, Edmond Hamilton, William L. Hamling, John and Evelyn Hatcher, Robert A. Heinlein, William F. Jenkins, Henry Kuttner, Fritz Leiber, Willy Ley, Frank Belknap Long, Robert W. Lowndes, and Dorothy McIlwraith.

Our thanks also go to Scott Meredith, P. Schuyler Miller, Samuel Mines, Catherine L. Moore, Sam Moskowitz, Marione R. Nickles, Raymond A. Palmer, John R. Pierce, Frederik Pohl, Fletcher Pratt, James L. Quinn, Malcolm Reiss, Darrell C. Richardson, Ross Rocklynne, Eric Frank Russell, Larry T. Shaw, Clifford D. Simak, Kenneth F. Slater, Clark Ashton Smith, Edward E. Smith, George O. Smith, Theodore H. Sturgeon, James V. Taurasi, Oswald Train, A. E. van Vogt, Manly Wade Wellman, James A. Williams, Robert Moore Williams, Jack Williamson, Joseph A. Winter, and Elinor Yocom.

In addition, we received many valuable suggestions for the revised edition from Poul Anderson, Charles and Dena Brown, Jack Chalker, Richard H. Eney, Ursula K. Le Guin, Sanford Meschkow, Larry Niven, Andre Norton, J. B. Post, Elliot K. Shorter, and David J. Williams, III.

The authors thank Coward-McCann, Inc. for permission to use passages from their symposium *Modern Science Fiction*; and Better Publications, Inc., for permission to quote from an editorial in *Startling Stories* for October 1952.

Special mention should be made of Ann and Frank Dietz who combined their talents as typesetters with their enthusiasm for and knowledge of the genre of imaginative fiction to produce a book of which the authors are justly proud.

L. Sprague de Camp and Catherine Crook de Camp
Villanova, Pennsylvania, July 1975

THE WORLD
OF IMAGINATIVE FICTION

In the twelvemonth that began in the autumn of 1938, science fiction burst upon the consciousness of the American people.

The idea was not new. Most readers had heard of H. G. Wells and Jules Verne. Many had read their stories or seen movies made from them. Some had noticed the growing number of pulp magazines with titles indicating wonder, astonishment, and amazement. The typical cover bore a startling picture of a hero in riding boots and, sometimes, headgear like a diver's helmet, a heroine in an abbreviated Mardi-gras costume, and a bug-eyed monster menacing both.

In October 1938, four such magazines were already established—*Amazing Stories, Astounding Stories, Thrilling Wonder Stories,* and *Weird Tales.* A fifth, *Marvel Science Stories,* was being launched.

But it was an event unrelated to publishing that gave the greatest momentum to speculative fiction. At 8:00 p.m., on the evening of October 30, 1938, the twenty-three-year-old Orson Welles staged the first radio broadcast of H. G. Wells's 1898 story, *The War of the Worlds.* The script, updating the original tale, told of the landing in New Jersey of a missile from Mars. The Martians emerge, and the radio audience hears the announcer's horrified voice shouting:

"Good heavens, something's wriggling out of the shadow like a gray snake. Now it's another one, and another. They look like tentacles to me. There,

[1]

I can see the thing's body. It's large as a bear, and it glitters like wet leather. But the face—it's indescribable. The eyes are black and gleam like a serpent. The mouth is V-shaped with saliva dripping from its rimless lips that seem to quiver and pulsate. . . . Wait! Something's happened!" (Hissing sound, followed by a rising hum.) "A small humped shape is rising out of the pit. I can make out a small gleam of light against a mirror. What's that? There's a jet of flame springing from that mirror and it leaps right at the advancing men. It strikes them head on. Good Lord, they're turning into flame! Now the whole field's caught fire. The woods. The barns. It's coming this way!" (Crash, followed by silence.)[1]

The Martians are conquering the earth with heat rays and other super-weapons when they succumb to Terran bacteria.

Listeners had been prepared for such an event by prophecies of air attack in the approaching Second World War. Thinking that they were hearing a broadcast of real events, some ran screaming into the streets or drove madly away. Reserve officers called their headquarters to ask for orders.

Afterwards, the broadcasters sheepishly apologized. In England, cantankerous old H. G. Wells testily termed the stunt an "outrage."

For science fiction, however, the event was a turning point. Many who had never read Wells's stories hunted them up. Others bought copies of those magazines with the bug-eyed monster covers. Sometimes they turned back the covers to hide the nature of their purchases, but they bought.

Soon, seven more science-fiction magazines were launched. On July 2, 1939, the First World Science Fiction Convention met at Caravan Hall on East 59th Street, New York City. Two hundred fans gathered from all over the United States and Canada. Two from California, Forrest J. Ackerman and "Morojo" (Myrtle Douglas) showed up in Martian-style tights and cloaks of emerald silk. The Futurian Society, a group of left-wing fans from Brooklyn, appeared with pamphlets denouncing the "dictatorship" of the "ruthless scoundrels" running the convention. Denied admission by the "scoundrels" (three muscular young fans named Moskowitz, Sykora, and Taurasi) they retired to a bar to brood on capitalistic injustice.

In the hall, notables (sixteen professional authors and five editors) were introduced. The guest of honor, veteran illustrator Frank R. Paul, was hailed, and the old German silent film, *Metropolis,* was shown. Speeches, auctions, and parties continued for three days.

Time wrote up the convention, noting its more juvenile aspects.[2] In the September issue of *Harper's,* Bernard De Voto, in his "Easy Chair" column, took a sharp and not friendly look at the phenomenon. After summarizing some recent stories, he wrote:

> This besotted nonsense is from the group of magazines known as the science pulps, which deal with both the World and the Universe of To-morrow and, as our items show, take no great pleasure in either. . . . The science discussed is idiotic beyond any possibility of exaggeration, but the point is that in this kind of fiction the bending of light or Heisenberg's formula is equivalent to the sheriff of the horse opera fanning his gun, the heroine of the sex pulp taking off her dress.[3]

Conceding that the stories were at least better-written than most Westerns, De Voto noted the crudity of most of the characterization and the strong vein of pessimism in many of the stories. He continued: "It is easy enough to classify these exhibits as paranoid phantasies converted into fiction for the titillation of tired, dull, or weak minds," but they merely reflected the interests and anxieties of their age.

Despite this blast, science fiction continued to expand. In 1939, August Derleth and Donald Wandrei announced the formation of their own publishing firm, Arkham House, to publish the books of the late fantasy-writer H. P. Lovecraft. Arkham House was the first of a number of small, semi-professional, specialist houses devoted entirely to imaginative fiction. The others began to appear in the late

1940s. Most of them struggled along for a few years and then vanished; but at this writing, Arkham House is still in business.

The fans continued to hold conventions—Chicago in 1940 and Denver in 1941. Several major publishers issued imaginative novels and short-story anthologies as cloth-bound books. The magazines proliferated until by 1941 there were twenty-one.

The Second World War severely limited science fiction publication and fan activity. As soon as the war ended, however, the number of magazines again swelled to over twenty. More book publishers added lines of imaginative fiction. The fans resumed their conventions. Movies, radio, and television devoted more and more attention to entertainment of this kind. Imaginative fiction enjoyed an expansion like that of the detective story after the First World War. Many leading magazines, such as *The New Yorker, The New Republic,* and *Life,* ran articles on the genre.

The Kremlin paid its own tribute. In the *Literaturnaya Gazyeta,* Bolkhovitinov and Zakharchenko told how the "lackey of Wall Street in the livery of a science-fiction writer" seduces his readers with the "wolf-pack laws of capitalism" and "unbridled racial propaganda" in order to "pervert and stultify their readers," thus betraying "the incurable disease of the capitalistic system."[4] Subsequently, writers in the Soviet Union themselves produced a respectable body of science fiction.

☆ ☆ ☆

Much ink has been expended in trying to define "science fiction" and "fantasy." As a practical matter, we can divide all fiction into two classes: realistic and imaginative. Realistic fiction, let us agree, consists of stories laid in the known world, either in the present or in the historical past. It tells of people like real human beings, doing the ordinary things that real people do. Realistic fiction does not tell of events that *actually* happened, or it would not be fiction. But, as far as the reader knows, the events *could* have happened.

Then let us use "imaginative fiction" for stories that could not have happened. They may be laid in the future, which has not yet come to pass, or on another world, or in the prehistoric past, about which nobody has detailed information. Or they contain elements like ghosts and magic, which most readers do not really believe in.

There is no sharp line between these two classes. For instance, many stories, otherwise realistic, have been laid in an imaginary country, like the Balkan kingdom of Ruritania in Anthony Hope's *The Prisoner of Zenda* (1894). Sinclair Lewis even made up an imaginary American state, Winnemac, for his novels satirizing Midwestern ways.

Anyone can open an atlas to prove that no such place exists. That, however, is to be like the literal-minded German publisher, who, offered Tolkien's fairy tale *The Hobbit,* turned it down on the ground that his people had searched dictionaries and encyclopedias, and there was no such thing as a Hobbit. Any fiction involves some make-believe, and one incapable of flights of fancy had better stick to non-fiction.

Moreover, a story may be realistic to one reader and imaginative to another, depending on his beliefs about reality. To a firm believer in ghosts, a ghost story is "realistic." He can accept an imaginary being like a ghost or an imaginary place like Ruritania as easily as an imaginary character like the hero of a realistic story. The difference between realistic and imaginative fiction is one of degree rather than of kind.

Likewise, no sharp line divides the two branches of imaginative fiction: science fiction and fantasy. In general, we use the term "fantasy" for stories based upon supernatural ideas or assumptions, such as the existence of demons, ghosts, witches, and workable magical spells. "Science fiction," on the other hand, is the term used for stories based upon scientific or pseudo-scientific ideas, such as revolutionary new inventions, life in the future, or life on other worlds. Some stories, like several of H. P. Lovecraft's, fall on the border between the two classes.

Whether the things in the story are possible does not necessarily tell us which class a story belongs in. There is more evidence for the existence of werewolves than there is for the possibility of time travel. Yet a werewolf story is classed as a fantasy, while a time-travel tale is considered science fiction. Neither is much more unlikely than the assumptions often met in detective stories, such as the eccentric old lady who always stumbles upon cooling corpses and solves the mystery after the bungling police have failed.

☆ ☆ ☆

If we study the history of fiction, we see a curious thing. Nearly all the stories that were told around primitive campfires, in ancient royal palaces, or in medieval castles and huts were what we now call imaginative fiction. Before 1700, realistic fiction—stories of ordinary people doing ordinary things—practically did not exist. Save for a few scattered early examples, it is only within the past three centuries that realistic fiction has come into being, become widely popular, and developed into the main kind of fictional entertainment; hence its current name of "mainstream fiction." To this day, however, imaginative fiction continues to thrive alongside its younger competitor.

Imaginative fiction took shape in the myths and legends of ancient times and of primitive peoples. These tales of gods and heroes were passed around by word of mouth because people had not yet learned to write.

In their most primitive form, myths and legends are often childishly irrational and exuberantly inconsistent and contradictory. As barbarism gropes towards civilization, bards piece this amorphous mass of fictions together and iron out the most obvious inconsistencies. The resulting unified narratives usually take the form of long narrative poems or epics, like the *Iliad,* the *Mahābhārata,* and the *Völsunga Saga.*

These poems were composed in fixed forms—that is, their lines had fixed lengths, rhythm, and sometimes rhyme. These devices made the stories much easier to memorize than they would otherwise have been, so that the unwritten tribal lore could be passed down without loss from one generation to the next. The current fashion in poetry is for free verse, with neither rhyme nor rhythm; but, because fixed-form poetry is so much easier to remember, the vast mass of free verse now being ground out will probably be forgotten a century hence, while people will still remember such rhythmic poems as "Half a league,/Half a league,/Half a league onward. . . ."

The early epics are full of details that modern readers recognize as elements of science fiction or fantasy. In Homer's *Odyssey,* composed about 800 B.C., the witch Circe turns the companions of Odysseus into pigs, and Odysseus has to threaten her with his sword to make her turn them back. Modern robots had a fictional forebear in Talos, a bronzen giant who ran round and round the island of Crete, throwing boulders at unwanted visitors.

As reading and writing developed, a class of literary men appeared. Some, tired of copying and recopying ancient epics, decided to write similar compositions of their own. These tales, imitating the traditional form, are called pseudo-epics or romances. About 20 B.C. the Roman poet Virgil (Publius Vergilius Maro) wrote his *Aenid* in imitation of the *Odyssey*. A little over a thousand years later, a Welsh monk, Geoffrey of Monmouth, wrote a *History of the Kings of Britain* in imitation of Virgil.

When literary men realized that their work would survive even if they did not put it into verse, the romance evolved into the novel—a book-length prose narrative, with a unified plot about a limited group of characters. The novel made its first appearance in Hellenistic Alexandria under the rule of the Ptolemies—the Macedonian kings of Egypt—during the three centuries before the Christian Era. The novel continued to flourish during the Classical or Graeco-Roman Era. It took the form of such works as Heliodoros' *Aithiopika,* which set a long-lived story pattern about the trials of a pair of sundered lovers, and the *Metamorphoses* of Lucius Apuleius. Apuleius was a Tunisian who wrote, in turgid Latin, a lively, humorous tale (better known under its later title, *The Golden Ass*) that approximates the sophisticated modern fantasy.

☆ ☆ ☆

Among the Greeks, many science-fictional ideas took shape. Late in the fifth century B.C., the Athenian playwright Aristophanes invented the mad scientist. In his play *The Clouds,* he introduced a character named Socrates, who was a caricature of the real philosopher of that name. In another play, *The Birds,* Aristophanes conceived the earth satellite vehicle. Two Athenian adventurers persuade the birds to build them an aerial city, Cloudcuckooland, by which they plan to cut off traffic between the gods in heaven and mortals on earth and thus extort favors from the gods.

The philosopher Plato, a younger contemporary of Aristophanes and a pupil of the real Socrates, also set forth science-fictional ideas. He wrote dialogues, or little plays, about his old teacher. In these, Plato told of caverns and tunnels inside the earth and of islands floating in the sky. In *Gorgias* he mentions the Isles of the Blest in the mysterious West. The *Politikos* tells of the Golden Age of King Kronos. This lasted until Zeus relaxed his grip on the universe, which then fell into ruin because of the growth of materialism. The *Republic* described the first known utopia—that is, a perfect, ideal commonwealth.

Most famous of Plato's imaginary places was his lost continent of Atlantis. His *Timaios* and *Kritias* tell of a large island in the Atlantic, ruled by the descendants of Poseidon from the rich city of Atlantis. The Atlanteans, said Plato, set out to conquer the Mediterranean region 9,000 years earlier but were repulsed by the Athenians of that elder day. Then Zeus, to punish the Atlanteans for their sins, sank the continent beneath the sea.

Although Plato's contemporaries paid little attention to his Atlantis yarn, mostly assuming it to be just one more political allegory, in modern times a cult has grown up around the concept. The modern Atlantists accept Plato's story as more or less literally true and search for Atlantis everywhere from Spitzbergen to Ceylon. The lost continent has also become a standard theme of modern imaginative fiction. Scores of stories have been laid in Atlantis or have brought Atlanteans down to modern times.

Interplanetary space opera began in the second century of the Christian Era with Loukianos of Samosata, or Lucian the Scoffer. In his *True History,* Loukianos wrote of a shipload of voyagers carried into the heavens by a whirlwind. There they become involved in a war between the king of the sun and the king of the moon over the colonization of Venus.

THE WORLD OF IMAGINATIVE FICTION

☆ ☆ ☆

After the West Roman Empire fell to the barbarians in the fifth century of the Christian Era, literacy in Europe all but vanished. For several centuries, most fiction took the form of the imaginary lives of saints. These hagiographies included tales of a whole class of martyrs who, after being beheaded, went about carrying their heads in their hands.

During the Dark Ages, civilization continued as before in the Near and Middle East, India, and China; but, because of poor communications, the writings of these lands had but little effect on barbarous Europe. At this time, however, writers set down many traditional tales told among the barbarians on the fringes of the former Roman Empire. Thus the Scandinavian sagas, the German *Niebelungenlied* and stories of Dietrich of Bern, the Welsh *White Book of Rhydderch* and *Red Book of Hergest,* and the Irish epics of the Red Branch and the voyage of Maelduin were saved from oblivion. Sometimes the old stories were given a thin Christian veneer to protect them from destruction by the Church.

With the revival of European learning after the eleventh century, some of the earlier literature was copied and circulated. Inspired by Virgil and others, European storytellers began composing their own romances, of which more than a hundred appeared in the next few centuries. Anyone who wants to read of parfit gentle knights rescuing maydenes faire from vile enchauntours can find here material to occupy his reading time for years.

Among these romances were tales of the more or less legendary King Arthur and his knights of the Table Round who, according to the romancers, lived, wooed, and wassailed like medieval knights some 600 years before the Age of Chivalry commenced. Others told of Arthur's adviser Merlin, the prototype of the good magician, the wise old white wizard, who appears so often in fantasy to this day.

Another legend cycle dealt with Charlemagne and his twelve paladins. An outstanding work of this group is the *Orlando Furioso* ("Mad Roland") written in the early 1500s by Ludovico Ariosto and later imitated by Edmund Spenser in his *Faerie Queene*. The *Orlando Furioso* revived the old theme of a voyage to the moon; one of Ariosto's heroes flies thither on the back of a hippogryff.

☆ ☆ ☆

The medieval romance came to an ignominious end about 1600. A Spaniard, Miguel de Cervantes, had fought against the Turks in the great naval battle of Lepanto and had been wounded there. Later, he was captured and enslaved by the Moors. Having led a rough, adventurous life, Cervantes knew that real adventures were seldom so picturesque, sanitary, and enjoyable as those of the romances. So he wrote a long novel, *Don Quixote de la Mancha,* about a woolly-minded would-be knight. This work so hilariously burlesqued the medieval romance that nobody thereafter dared to write one.

Freed from the conventions of the traditional romance, writers continued to play with imaginative ideas. A century after Sir Thomas More's *Utopia* (1516) had revived the theme of the perfect society, Sir Francis Bacon, influenced both by Plato and by More, pictured another flawless civilization in *The New Atlantis.* About the same time, a Dominican friar from Calabria, Tommaso Campanella, wrote a similar work while spending twenty-eight years in jail for a plot to free Naples from the Spaniards. His book, *The City of the Sun,* described an ideal commonwealth in Ceylon. Like Bacon's New Atlanteans, the people are very scientific; like Plato's Republicans they practice communism of women and children.

Stories of marvelous journeys and voyages continued as popular as they had been for thousands of years. In the seventeenth and eighteenth centuries, there were plenty of regions of the earth unexplored by Europeans and therefore plausible sites for the fantastic cities and islands of the storytellers. In *Gulliver's Travels* (1726), Jonathan Swift sent his hero on voyages to the Pacific Ocean. There he found a land of giants, a land of midgets, a land of civilized horses, and a flying island. Swift used these conceits to satirize human nature and certain aspects of life in the eighteenth century.

Stories were also written about flying, about journeys to

the moon, and about trips through those hollows inside the earth of which Plato had written. Robert Paltock, in *The Life and Adventures of Peter Wilkins* (1751), and Ludvig Baron von Holberg in *Nicholas Klim* (1741) sent their heroes into the earth's interior. Paltock's hero finds a race of winged folk living in an immense cavern and marries a flying woman. Holberg, sometimes called the founder of Danish literature, made the earth's interior hollow, with an internal sun. The idea has been used by many more recent writers, such as Victor Rousseau in *The Eye of Balamok* (1920) and Edgar Rice Burroughs in his stories of Pellucidar. It is too bad that the laws of physics make the scheme impractical.

Among the moon-journey stories, the astronomer Johannes Kepler told of being ferried to the moon by friendly demons. Francis Godwin sent his hero to the same place in a sedan chair powered by trained birds.

It remained for Cyrano de Bergerac to hit upon the one method that works. Cyrano, when not fighting duels with people who made remarks about his nose, was a prolific and intelligent writer. In his posthumously published *Voyage dans la lune* (1657), Cyrano (who influenced Swift) devised some whimsical methods of flight. One was to gather dew in vials and let the sun shine on them; for everybody knows that the sun sucks up the dew. But finally his hero reached the moon in a "flying chariot" with mechanical wings, propelled by skyrockets. Thus Cyrano anticipated the modern rocket-powered space ship.

When it became generally known that the earth was only one of a family of planets circling the sun, the question naturally arose: were the other planets inhabited? In "Micromegas" (1752), Voltaire brought to earth an eight-mile-high visitor from Sirius and a slightly smaller native of Saturn. Because of their size, these beings have a hard time deciding whether there is intelligent life on earth.

☆ ☆ ☆

Aside from some ghost stories, tales of witchcraft, and religious tracts, few supernatural fantasies were written in the seventeenth and early eighteenth centuries. Cervantes had slain the medieval romance. Moreover, after 1650 came a general decline in belief in the supernatural. The eighteenth century saw the growth of a skeptical, rationalistic, materialistic outlook. It also saw the rise of the realistic novel, of which Daniel Defoe's *Robinson Crusoe* (1719) was one of the first. Books for children, pioneered by John Bunyan in the seventeenth century, also began to be written, although for a long time they consisted of grimly moralistic tales with a maximum of uplift and a minimum of entertainment.

In the eighteenth and early nineteenth centuries, however, fantasy reëntered the stream of European fiction. It sprang from three sources. One was the oriental extravaganza. In 1704 a French scholar, Antoine Galland, found an Arabic manuscript containing tales of Sindbad the Sailor. After he had translated them into French, Galland learned that these stories were part of a much larger collection called *The Arabian Nights* or, more accurately, *The Thousand and One Nights.* These stories, mostly composed in Egypt between the years 900 and 1400, have since been translated into many European languages.

Another source of modern fantasy was the Gothic novel, invented in Germany and introduced to England by Horace Walpole's *The Castle of Otranto* (1764). This lively and still surprisingly readable novel of medieval murder and spookery has all the elements that became standard props of the Gothic horror story: an Italian locale, a lecherous tyrant, an imperiled virgin, an impoverished young hero of noble blood, a monk, a castle with trapdoors and secret passages, eldritch legends, a ruined monastery, and *two* ghosts. Who could ask for more?

Otranto was followed by a flood of Gothic novels in England and Germany: by William Beckford's *Vathek* (1786) about a caliph who, avid for power and knowledge, sells himself to the Evil One; by *The Mysteries of Udolpho* and others by Mrs. Ann Radcliffe in the 1790s; by Charles Maturin's endless *Melmoth the Wanderer* (1820); and by many others.

The best-remembered of all is *Frankenstein* (1818) by Mary Wollstonecraft Godwin, mistress and later wife of the poet Shelley. In this tale, a Swiss medical student, Victor Frankenstein, assembles a synthetic man from medical specimens and graveyard corpses and brings it to life. Frankenstein (sometimes confused in popular folklore with his monster) is a typical hero of the Romantic Era: weepy, swooning, hypersensitive, and ineffectual, rather like Shelley himself.

When the monster comes to life, Frankenstein flees in terror, leaving his creation to fend for itself. The story tells of the monster's revenge on its faithless creator. Mary Shelley's melancholy, murderous monster is the ancestor of all the robots and androids that shamble through modern science fiction.

The third source of modern fantasy was the fairy tale. In medieval and later times, the European peasantry continued to hand down traditional stories, just as they had before the rise of Western civilization. In the early 1800s, people like the Grimm brothers in Germany and Hans Christian Andersen in Denmark began to collect such folk tales. Later, other writers like Lewis Carroll and George Macdonald began composing original stories in this genre.

☆ ☆ ☆

During the nineteenth century, many writers like Hawthorne, Melville, and Bulwer-Lytton tried their hands at an occasional imaginative story. Dickens introduced the theme of time travel in *A Christmas Carol* (1843). Edward Everett Hale described an artificial earth satellite vehicle in his short story "The Brick Moon."

The main development of the century, as far as imaginative fiction is concerned, was the discovery that one could make a living by writing such stories.

A frail, moody, unstable, American genius, Edgar Allan Poe (1809-49), pioneered the detective story and, with some of his fellow writers, gave the short story its modern form. Many of his stories are plain Gothic horror tales, or labored, dismal attempts at jocular humor; but about a dozen clearly belong to imaginative fiction. He wrote stories about hypnotism, alchemy, a flight to the moon, and a transatlantic balloon flight in the year 2848.

Poe borrowed some ideas from stories that had appeared in the British *Blackwood's Magazine,* but his vivid and forceful treatment made the resulting tales seem original. He advanced the art of fiction by eliminating the rambling digressions and moralistic platitudes that had cluttered up stories, and by following his assumptions to their logical conclusions, regardless of fictional conventions.

Poe's novel *The Narrative of A. Gordon Pym* takes its hero to an island in the South Pacific, where the natives are terrified of anything white and the water can literally be split with a knife. Escaping, the traveler sails on to Antarctica, which consists of a huge, horizon-wide cataract of white vapor falling into the sea. There the story ends. A postscript explains that Mr. Pym died before he could complete his account, although that sounds like a mere excuse on Poe's part for his not finishing the story. Other writers have composed sequels to it.

After Poe died, his work came to the notice of the French writer Charles Baudelaire, a leader of the group that called themselves the Decadents. Fascinated, Baudelaire translated Poe's works into French in the 1850s and 60s. This translation much impressed an unsuccessful young French lawyer, stockbroker, and playwright named Jules Verne (1828-1905).

Inspired by Poe and other contemporary novelists, Verne became the world's first full-time science-fiction writer. He composed nearly a hundred novels, some simply tales of travel and adventure but most based upon scientific speculation. Most of his stories take the form of a marvelous journey, on which the author has sent along one or two learned characters to explain the wonders of science to the other characters and to the reader. Verne sent his people around the world in a submarine in *Twenty Thousand Leagues Under the Sea* (1870); into Plato's "hollows inside the earth" in *A Journey to the Center of the Earth* (1864); and around the moon in a huge artillery shell in *From the Earth to the Moon* (1865).

Verne is often cited, not only as the "father" of science fiction but also as a prophet of scientific advances. It has been said (wrongly) that an inventor was denied a patent on a periscope because Verne had already described the device. Actually, Verne was a cautious prophet, who read the technical literature of his time and applied his readings to his stories. Thus, when he speculated about submarines, some of the world's navies were just beginning to experiment with them. His stories have little characterization or plot but much lively action, Gallic wit, and good-natured satire on the supposed characteristics of various nationalities.

☆ ☆ ☆

As the nineteenth century ended and the twentieth began, several eminent authors ventured into the field of imaginative fiction. Rudyard Kipling's "With the Night Mail" (1909) told of future transatlantic air service. His flying machines are not at all like those of today, but that is the chance one takes in predicting tomorrow's inventions.

H. Rider Haggard wrote over fifty adventure novels, many on the lost-race theme. His explorer-heroes usually visit Africa and find a mysterious city inhabited by folk descended from a vanished civilization. Haggard had the advantage of knowing Africa at first hand, having worked there as a young man in the civil service. He also had considerable sympathy with the native Africans.

Likewise Sir Arthur Conan Doyle, when not writing medieval romances or stories about Sherlock Holmes, had a try at imaginative tales. His most successful was *The Lost World* (1912), in which a party of explorers ascend an almost inaccessible plateau in South America. There they find ape-men along with dinosaurs and other extinct animals. The novel, which introduced the gorilla-like Professor Challenger—one of the immortal characters of science fiction—has been made into a motion picture at least twice, each with a cast of rubber dinosaurs lumbering jerkily about the scene. Doyle's imaginary plateau is based upon the real Mount Roraima in South America. Alas, when Roraima was scaled, it was found to harbor no dinosaurs or toxodonts, only some interesting species of small birds and squirrels.

The brightest name in imaginative fiction after Verne, however, is that of Herbert George Wells (1866-1946).

Reared in poverty, H. G. Wells worked as a draper's helper and briefly attended the Royal College of Science on a scholarship. There he heard lectures from Thomas Huxley, who had been one of Darwin's leading backers.

Wells went into teaching, journalism, and at last into free-lance writing, where he had a quick success. He wrote over eighty books, including realistic novels, tracts, essays, and popularizations of science and history. His main contributions to imaginative fiction were made from 1895 to 1914.

In one of Wells's first stories, *The Time Machine* (1895), an inventor sends himself nearly a million years into the future. He finds that man has evolved into two new species, the delicate Eloi, descended from the former upper classes, and the gnomelike Morlocks, descended from the workers. The Morlocks feed the Eloi but eat them in return. Fleeing the Morlocks, the traveler goes ahead thirty million years. He finds himself at last on a desolate beach, lit by a huge, immobile, red, horizon-hung sun; for the earth has stopped rotating. Nothing lives save an octopuslike thing flopping on a sandbank. Filled with horror, the traveler returns to his own time.

Other stories by Wells forecast the air age and future war. A short story, "The Land Ironclads" (1903) anticipated the military tank. A novel, *The World Set Free* (1914), foresaw the atomic bomb—dropped, however, by hand from open-cockpit airplanes.

After the First World War, although Wells could still tell a good story when he chose, his writings became so laden with arguments for the causes he deemed worthy—Socialism, peace, democracy, science, education, conservation, sexual freedom, and population control—that the propaganda drowned the story.

Wells grew up at a time when many intellectuals hailed a combination of science and Socialism as the cure for all the ills of mankind. Wells himself adopted this view. In 1888 an American, Edward Bellamy, wrote a novel called *Looking Backward, 2000-1887,* which also preached this doctrine.

Although very successful in its time, Bellamy's novel seems

unreadably dull today. For one thing, after Bellamy has put his hero to sleep in 1887 and awakened him in 2000, nothing happens except that the hero listens to endless lectures on the social and economic organization of that future time. For another, science and Socialism have both been tried on a large scale during the present century, and neither seems the cure-all that its prophets predicted.

Science-fiction stories preaching Socialism brought a reaction in the form of stories preaching against Socialism. David M. Parry's *The Scarlet Empire* (1906) sends its hero to the bottom of the sea, where he finds the people of the lost Atlantis living under a huge glass dome. The Atlanteans have so strictly egalitarian a Socialism that everyone must wear the same clothes and eat the same food. Each is allowed so many spoken words a day and wears a gadget around his neck to count the words and prevent cheating.

Even more ironic, in the light of hindsight, was Victor Rousseau's *The Messiah of the Cylinder* (1917). This novel foresaw a Britain ruled by an atheistic Socialist tyranny, which encourages such horrors as divorce and birth control. The pious Christian Russians, however, come to the aid of the oppressed Good People, destroy the Socialist armies in a war fought with death rays and airplanes that grapple each other with great steel jaws, and restore the ancient virtues.

There have also been a number of stories arguing against the whole Industrial Revolution. Among these were Samuel Butler's *Erewhon* (1872) and Robert Graves's *Watch the North Wind Rise* (1949). The weakness of their arguments lies in the fact that, if the world went back to pre-industrial technology, it could support only a fraction of its present population. Authors who preach "back to the hand loom and the horse-drawn plow" never explain what to do with the surplus people, although some uninhibited science-fiction writers have suggested eating them.

One of the most chilling warnings against mechanization of life appeared in the play *R. U. R.* (1921) by the Czech author and playwright Karel Čapek (pronounced CHAH-pek), who invented the word "robot." The initials stand for "Rossum's Universal Robots," the name of a company that makes synthetic men. These beings eventually revolt and destroy their human masters.

"Robot," from a Czech word meaning "servitude," was at once adopted into the English language. In present-day science fiction, however, the word "android" is generally used for a synthetic human being that, like Čapek's robots, looks like a real one. A "robot" is conceived as being a man-shaped machine, looking like L. Frank Baum's Tin Woodman.

Thus have ancient bards and poets and modern story-tellers dreamed their wondrous dreams of humanoid machines, travel through space and time, supermen and superwomen, talking animals, invaders from other worlds, and all the rest. Thus in the twentieth century has fantasy's offspring, science fiction, come of age. Cradled in Greece, child of the Middle Ages, youthfully adventurous in the early days of the Industrial Revolution, this literature of ideas has matured into an endlessly fascinating, powerful force that stimulates the weakest imagination and kindles the meanest spirit.

MODERN IMAGINATIVE FICTION

From 1890 on, the habit of reading magazines grew and their number and circulation rose accordingly. By 1900, several general-circulation magazines published occasional imaginative fiction. Thus Wells's "The Land Ironclads" appeared in *The Strand* for December 1903, along with one of Conan Doyle's stories of Sherlock Holmes.

In the early 1900s, the Munsey Company's magazines, such as *Munsey's Magazine, The Argosy, All-Story Weekly,* and *Cavalier,* published a distinguished list of such "different" stories, as they called them. In 1912 appeared in *All-Story* the first successful novel by one of the most voluminous writers of the entire genre. The story was "Under the Moons of Mars," by "Norman Bean."[1] The author was a Westerner in his thirties, who had tried without success several occupations, including bookkeeper, cowboy, and railroad detective. Once when he read a magazine story that struck him as especially bad, he swore that he could do better. Thus did Edgar Rice Burroughs (1875-1950) write his first story. In 1917, the story was republished in book form, under the writer's true name, as *A Princess of Mars.*

John Carter, an adventurer and professional soldier who cannot remember his childhood, is mustered out of the defeated Confederate Army and goes west to try prospecting. Trapped in a cave by Apaches, he hears a rustling noise behind him and finds himself paralyzed. After looking into the cave, the Indians flee in terror. Watching them go, Carter sees the planet Mars on the horizon. He focuses his will upon it—and finds himself standing naked on the moss-covered dead sea bottoms of Mars.

Soon, Carter is captured by four-armed green men fifteen feet tall, with eyes at the sides of their heads. Mars harbors other humanoid races, and Carter falls in love with a fellow captive, a beautiful princess of the red race, a race altogether manlike except that they lay eggs. Life on Burroughs's Mars, with its four-armed giants and its boat-shaped aircraft propelled by the Eighth Barsoomian Ray, is suspiciously like life in Atlantis and Lemuria as described by the Theosophists, Helena P. Blavatsky and William Scott-Elliot.

This was the first of ten[2] Martian novels: *The Gods of Mars, The Warlord of Mars,* and so on. In 1934, Burroughs started a companion series: *Pirates of Venus* and its successors. These, however, never had quite the grip of his Martian stories.

Right after "Under the Moons of Mars," Burroughs published, in *All-Story* for October 1912, the most popular tale he ever wrote: *Tarzan of the Apes.* When this appeared as a book in 1914, it made Burroughs's fortune. Tarzan became the hero not only of more than a score of books but also of a long series of movies and comic strips. The town that grew up around Burroughs's ranch in California was named Tarzana, and there is a Tarzan, Texas.

Tarzan is an English boy, brought up by African apes of a species unknown to science. Kipling read and liked the yarn, supposing that Burroughs had paid him the compliment of imitation. Burroughs, however, swore that, when he wrote *Tarzan,* he had never heard of the *Jungle Books* and their wolf-reared hero Mowgli. He credited his inspiration to the Roman legend of Romulus and Remus. But Burroughs never admitted getting ideas for his Barsoom from the Theosophists, either, although the resemblances seem too close for coincidence.

In the magazine version of *Tarzan of the Apes* appeared a character called "Sabor the Tiger." H. P. Lovecraft, then a semi-invalided youth, wrote a letter to the magazine, pointing out that there are no tigers in Africa. Thus, in the book,

Sabor became a lioness.

From 1914 to 1939, Burroughs brought out a Tarzan book almost every year, until there were twenty-two of them. Tarzan grows to invincible manhood, acquires a veneer of civilization, and learns that he is really Lord Greystoke. He marries Jane Porter, the daughter of an English missionary, and obtains an "empire" in Africa and a son.

Many of the stories are based on the lost-race theme. Tarzan blunders into some lost city inhabited by Atlanteans, or ancient Romans, or ape-men left over from the Pleistocene. He is captured and imprisoned, escapes, is recaptured and forced to fight in the arena, escapes again, and so on. When he is not finding lost cities, the kidnapping of Jane by Arabs or other ill-wishers gives him an excuse to haul out his old leopard-skin loin cloth and go swinging off from branch to branch.

Burroughs also wrote other imaginative novels, laid on the moon, inside a hollow earth, or on an unknown island in the Pacific. Compared with the work of such finished and cerebral writers as H. G. Wells and Fowler Wright, this vast mass of picaresque adventure-romance is pretty thin stuff. Burroughs admitted that he owed the sale of over 35,000,000 copies of his books—and that before the days of cheap paperbacks—to his care never to subject his readers' minds to the slightest strain. There is little characterization, save that heroes are heroic and villains villainous.

Burroughs cared little for scientific plausibility or even for internal consistency. Although his Martians have radium rifles that shoot by radar sights for hundreds of miles, they prefer to fight with swords and spears. Although they soar through the thin Martian air in boatlike "fliers," they have no better ground transport than chariots or eight-legged thoats.

Still, there are sound reasons for Burroughs's popularity. His books are excellent juveniles. Burroughs gets his action going right at the start and never slows down. The style of his early books is cluttered with some of the useless verbiage then deemed "fine writing," but it improved as he went along until he learned to write in good, brisk, straightforward English. He had imagination, ingenuity, and humor, and there is something charming about his unabashed romanticism, in which princesses are always beautiful. Parents need not fear that Burroughs will convert their young to the sexual revolution; in *Tarzan the Terrible,* after Tarzan has rescued his long-lost and beloved mate from perils dire and has taken her to a tree house he has built in the jungle, they spend their entire first night *talking.*

Despite his faults, there is much solid entertainment in Burroughs's works. His Mars, like Carroll's Looking-Glass Land and Howard's Hyborian Age, has the vividness that a potent imagination can impart to a fictional setting, so that its glamor lingers in the mind long after one has forgotten the author's shortcomings.

☆ ☆ ☆

The beginning of the twentieth century saw increasing specialization in magazines. The period also witnessed a considerable American literature of juvenile novels, some cloth-bound and some in the paperback "dime novel" format. Some had imaginative themes, such as William Wallace Cook's interplanetary story, *Adrift in the Unknown* (1904), and Victor Appleton's "Tom Swift" series starting in 1910.

Similar developments appeared in other countries. Before the First World War, German youth was absorbed in the doings of Captain Mors, a kind of paperbacked interplanetary Captain Nemo. But, while Europe has produced many imaginative stories in book form, some of the highest quality, it has never experienced a growth of specialized science-fiction magazines on a scale like that of the United States.

In 1904, a young inventor named Hugo Gernsback (1884-1967) arrived in New York City. Born in Luxemburg and educated in Germany, Gernsback set up an Electro Importing Company and four years later brought out a magazine called *Modern Electrics.* In the issue of April 1911, Gernsback (a short man with a large round head and a prominent nose) inserted among the engineering articles the first instalment of his *Ralph 124C 41+: A Romance of the Year 2660.*

Gernsback accented the "science" part of science fiction,

holding these stories to be a practical means of conveying scientific fact with a slight sugar-coating of fiction. He hoped thus to interest young readers in scientific careers and to stimulate the minds of scientists and inventors. He objected to giving the name "science fiction" to stories like Burroughs's tales of Barsoom, wherein a pseudo-scientific assumption was used as a peg on which to hang a picaresque adventure-romance.

Hence most of *Ralph 124C 41+* is a travelogue wherein Ralph, a super-scientist of his time, shows his sweetheart, Alice 212B 423, the wonders of New York, such as its germicidal Baccilatorium and its Hypnobioscopes, which teach while you sleep. Although the tale is unreadable today, the technological forecasts of Gernsback, who invented the word "television" long before the apparatus of that name came into use, were unusually shrewd.

During the next two decades, Gernsback published several similar magazines, such as *The Electrical Experimenter* and *Science and Invention*. All carried science fiction, which Gernsback called "scientifiction." He had trouble at first in getting authors to write under their real names, for they feared that writing such fiction was beneath their dignity. But humorist Ellis Parker Butler contributed, and Gernsback got novels from Ray Cummings, who had been Edison's secretary, and A. Merritt.

Cummings's *Tarrano the Conqueror* is typical. An ambitious Venerian[3] plots to seize the rule of Venus, the earth, and Mars by dangling before the peoples of those worlds the promise of immortality. After a monotonous series of captures and escapes, Tarrano is defeated in his Venerian polar citadel of ice and exiled to a planetoid. To a reader who has lived through the era of Hitler, Stalin, and the PLO, the surprising thing about this story is its gentleness. The characters pass up chances to kill their enemies in a way that seems absurd today.

By 1926, Gernsback felt able to start a magazine filled exclusively with science fiction. With the issue of April 1926, *Amazing Stories* was born.

This was not the only magazine devoted to imagination at

the time. In 1919, Street and Smith Publications had issued *Thrill Book,* which ran to sixteen issues before a combination of editorial inexperience and a printer's strike put it out of business. Then in March 1923, came *Weird Tales.*

☆ ☆ ☆

To consider *Weird Tales*'s contribution, we must go back a bit. During the nineteenth century, after the great Gothic outburst, fantasies continued to appear with little change. Pure fantasy has attracted the general-fiction writer more than has the science-fiction story, perhaps because a writer without technical knowledge feels better qualified to tackle a tale of the former class. Hence the many ghost stories by such writers as Dickens, Hawthorne, O. Henry, and Henry James.

Fitz-James O'Brien, a young Irish-American, had written only a few imaginative stories when he was killed in the Civil War, but those he had written were of a superior quality. In his short "What Was It?", a man in a haunted house is attacked by an invisible ghoul, which he subdues after a fearful struggle. The story foreshadows Maupassant's Horla and the similar creature in Ambrose Bierce's "What Was it?"

In O'Brien's "The Diamond Lens," a young microscopist makes contact with the spirit of Leeuwenhoek[4] through a Spiritualist medium. The spirit tells him that he can make a microscope of unsurpassed power by subjecting a large diamond to an electric current—Spiritualist mediums and electric currents being new and sensational in the 1850s. The microscopist does so, murdering a man to get the diamond. In a drop of water, he sees a beautiful woman, with whom he falls in love until the drop evaporates.

In the middle of the century, Alexandre Dumas *père* brought the werewolf theme into current fantastic literature in his novel *The Wolf Leader,* and the Irish writer Joseph Sheridan Le Fanu revived the vampire motif with his novella *Carmilla.* While less familiar than Bram Stoker's later *Dracula, Carmilla* introduces most of the standard elements of the vampire tale. Its ending, in which the vampire hunters open the grave of the Countess Mircalla, find a perfectly preserved corpse floating in blood, drive a stake through its heart, and cut off its head, reads like an imitation of all the vampire stories ever written. In fact, the imitation is the other way round. *Dracula* (1897), a much longer, more complex, and more powerful tale, uses the same elements more effectively.

Another imaginative writer of the time was Lord Bulwer-Lytton, whose novel *The Coming Race* took its hero underground into a cavern world. There he finds a race of supermen using a mentally dirigible force, *vril,* to blast rocks and monsters. Mme. Blavatsky adopted *vril* as part of her Theosophical scheme, averring that the Atlanteans had propelled their aircraft with this force. Bulwer-Lytton's other works include a celebrated ghost story, "The Haunters and the Haunted," and two influential novels of the occult, *Zanoni* (1842) and *A Strange Story* (1862). These books probably reflect the ideas of the French occultist Alphonse Louis Constant ("Eliphas Lévy"), with whom Bulwer-Lytton dabbled in magic. *Zanoni* tells of an English artist, Glyndon, who, while studying magic in Italy, rashly evokes a horrid female spook, the Dweller on the Threshold, that haunts him thereafter. The story probably inspired *The Lurker at the Threshold* (1945), begun by H. P. Lovecraft and finished by August Derleth.

In late Victorian times, the misanthropic Ambrose Bierce carried on the art of fantasy. Born in Ohio in 1842, Bierce fought in the Civil War and led a wandering journalistic life, much of it in San Francisco. In 1913, at seventy-one, he went to Mexico, apparently to report on Villa's revolutionists, and disappeared. Of the several stories of his end, a plausible one is that, disillusioned with Villa, he denounced the Mexican to his face as a bandit, and Villa simply told his men: "Shoot him!"

Bierce wrote many short horror stories, supernatural and otherwise. They are uneven, vigorous, crude, and rhetorically extravagant; in the typical "The Middle Toe of the Right Foot," a man is frightened to death by the ghost of a wife he murdered.

☆ ☆ ☆

While the Gothic novel was in bloom, Walter Scott launched the modern historical novel with his *Waverley*

(1814) and its numerous successors. Many earlier people had written stories laid in a time before their own; Homer's *Iliad* and Xenophon's *Youth of Cyrus* belong in this category. Such writers, however, had made no special point of the social differences between their own times and those of which they wrote; often they were not even aware of these differences.

Scott discovered not only that the past was different in many important ways from the present but also that these differences could be turned to fictional account. The costumes and customs of a bygone age had entertainment value in themselves. To an ordinary man in any civilization, harassed by the petty everyday needs of a drab existence, life in an earlier century seems more colorful and dramatic than that of his own world. Hence Scott looked back to the Middle Ages, just as medieval men looked back to Rome, the Romans to Greece, and the Greeks to the great days of Crete and Mycenae.

Scott's novels touched off a whole wave of medieval romanticism, which reached its climax in the Eglinton Tournament of 1839. Lord Eglinton, a likable and extravagant young peer, and his friends, at vast expense, staged the last authentic medieval tournament on Eglinton's Scottish estates. Alas for romance! It poured.

In the 1880s, William Morris (1834-96), the British artist, decorator, poet, reformer, Socialist, capitalist, publisher, printer, and novelist, revived heroic fantasy, moribund since the death of the medieval romance. Morris combined the antiquarian romanticism of Scott and his imitators with the supernaturalism of Horace Walpole and *his* imitators. During his last decade, Morris wrote seven novels of this type, to add to his numerous shorter and earlier writings.

Of the seven novels of Morris's late years, two, *The House of the Wulfings* and *The Roots of the Mountains*, are not properly fantastic. They are semi-historical tales, wherein improbably noble North European barbarians defend their homeland against cruel invaders, Romans in the first case and unnamed aggressors resembling Huns in the second. The remaining five novels, however, are all laid in imaginary pseudo-medieval worlds, where magic works.

Of these novels, the longest, *The Well at the World's End,* is probably the best and still fairly readable. The others tend to start well but become dull and prolix towards the end. Morris's stories suffered, not from Victorian prudery—his characters enjoy a good roll in the hay—but from Victorian optimism. His good people are too good and his bad ones not very bad. There is just too much sweetness and light for our disillusioned times. Still, Morris deserved credit for launching the modern heroic fantasy, which still thrives in Tolkien's *Lord of the Rings* and in the Conan stories by Howard, de Camp, and Carter.

☆ ☆ ☆

In the first quarter of the twentieth century, three men of the British Isles became the leaders of fantasy: an Englishman, Algernon Blackwood (1869-1951); a Welshman, Arthur Machen (1863-1950); and an Anglo-Irishman, Lord Dunsany[5] (1878-1958). Machen and Blackwood handled a variety of supernatural themes, such as ghosts, elemental spirits, and Elder Gods, with great competence and subtlety.

A dreamy, impractical person and a slow and painful writer, Machen never made a decent living from his writing or from anything else, although he tried clerking, teaching, reporting, and acting. Despite some irritating mannerisms and the vague inconclusiveness of many stories, Machen's work is a necessity for any connoisseur of fantasy. His favorite subject was the survival in Britain, in caves, cults, and covens, of pagan magic and fertility worship and of the spirits to whom these rites were addressed. His short story "The Bowmen" unintentionally started the legend of the angels of Mons in the First World War.

Blackwood spent some of his younger years in Canada and used his experience in some of his stories. *John Silence, Physician Extraordinary* (1908) introduces that now familiar fantasy hero: the professional ghost-catcher, who exorcises supernatural menaces. In this book, Doctor Silence copes with a ghost, a fire elemental, the wraiths of a gang of Satanists, and a case of lycanthropy.

Edward John Moreton Drax Plunkett, eighteenth Baron

Dunsany, wrote in a lighter vein and adapted the heroic fantasy, pioneered by William Morris in the 1880s, to the short-story form. A man of towering stature and an enthusiast for games and sports, from chess to lion-hunting, Dunsany traveled the world, made an abortive entry into British politics, and served with distinction in the Boer and First World Wars. Thereafter he lived alternately in a Regency house in Kent and an Irish castle an hour's drive from Dublin. When not chasing the fugitive fox with hounds and horn or gunning for snipe and other edible birds, he devoted himself to writing. He was briefly associated with William Butler Yeats and the Abbey Theatre in the Irish Renaissance.

Dunsany turned out over sixty volumes of stories, plays, poems, and autobiography, most of them written with a quill pen. Although his plays had considerable success—five were running at once on Broadway in the early 1920s—he was essentially a writer's writer. He strongly influenced other writers in the fantasy genre but never achieved best-sellerdom.

Lovecraft called Dunsany's work "Unexcelled in the sorcery of crystalline singing prose, and supreme in the creation of a gorgeous and languorous world of iridescently exotic vision. . . ."[6] which is pretty iridescent prose in itself. Some of Dunsany's stories are laid in Ireland, some in London, some in an Africa odder than anything Burroughs ever thought up, and some in never-never lands of his own creation. He throws off quotably epigrammatic sentences: "The Gibbelins eat, as is well known, nothing less good than man." "It does not become adventurers to care who eats their bones." "To be a god and to fail to achieve a miracle is a despairing sensation; it is as though among men one should determine upon a hearty sneeze and as though no sneeze should come. . . ."[7]

America produced one comparable fantasy writer during this time: James Branch Cabell (1879-1958), who wrote elegant fantasies about an imaginary Baroque land called Poictesme. The stories are full of genial cynicism, subtly ribald humor, and ironic comments on the war between the sexes. Cabell had been writing these novels for years without arousing much attention when John S. Sumner of the New York Society for the Suppression of Vice tried unsuccessfully to suppress Cabell's *Jurgen* (1919) for obscenity. Thereupon Cabell became famous and acquired a loyal following.

☆ ☆ ☆

After the failure of *Thrill Book,* the idea of a magazine of imaginative fiction next occurred to J. C. Henneberger, publisher of the successful *College Humor.* Henneberger was inspired to start *Weird Tales* by Poe's lines:

> From a wild weird clime that lieth, sublime
> Out of SPACE—out of TIME.

Henneberger hired Edwin F. Baird, a mystery writer, to edit *Weird Tales* and its companion *Detective Tales.* The first issue of *Weird Tales,* with a cover picture of a man and a woman writhing in the grip of a giant octopus, appeared with the date of March 1923. While the magazine ran both science fiction and fantasy, it published more of the latter.

H. P. Lovecraft was among the writers early enlisted, somewhat against his will, as regular contributors to *Weird Tales.* To Lovecraft at this time, writing was something a gentleman did for his own and his friends' entertainment, without thought of vulgar money. Starting with the issue of October 1923, however, Lovecraft appeared in nearly every issue for a year and a half. Many of the stories had previously been published in uncopyrighted amateur publications, but Baird paid for them anyway.

In 1924, however, the magazine ran into financial problems. Editing both *Weird Tales* and its companion magazine proved too much for Baird, and he and Henneberger parted company. By then, Henneberger was in debt to the extent of around half a hundred thousand dollars. Henneberger made tentative moves towards hiring Lovecraft as editor, either of *Weird Tales* or of a projected companion magazine. Horrified by the idea of moving to Chicago, where there was no Colonial architecture for him to admire, Lovecraft put Henneberger off, and nothing came of these plans.

In a complicated deal, Baird and another employee became the publishers of *Detective Tales,* while the management of *Weird Tales* was assumed by another employee and a new editor, Farnsworth Wright. A native of San Francisco, then living and writing in Chicago, Wright was a tall, gaunt Shakespearean scholar with Parkinson's disease. This affliction caused his fingers to twitch so uncontrollably that he had to type his signature on letters.

Despite this handicap and a low budget that forced him to print much inferior copy, Wright achieved such signal results that we can speak of a definite *Weird Tales* school of writing—or perhaps a Lovecraft school, Lovecraft being its leader and strongest influence.

Howard Phillips Lovecraft (1890-1937) was a lean, lantern-jawed man who lived most of his life in his native Providence, Rhode Island. His father died insane when he was a boy. His mother, a weepy psychoneurotic, coddled and overprotected her son until he grew up almost totally incapable of facing or coping with the world at large. Illnesses forced him out of school before he had completed his high-school courses. Their nature cannot now be certainly diagnosed, but rheumatic fever, hypothyroidism, and hypoglycaemia may be suspected.

Lovecraft spent his twenties as a sickly, eccentric recluse, staying home, doing no useful work, and reading widely. After his mother died, also insane, in 1921, he became more active and acquired a circle of friends and acquaintances in the amateur journalism movement. Eventually, in 1924, he married one of them, a bustling New York businesswoman and a divorcée seven years older than he, and moved to New York. It is curious that, on one hand, Lovecraft at this stage was subject to the most violent xenophobia and ethnocentrism, with the most bigoted prejudices against foreigners, immigrants, and ethnics, while on the other he married a woman of Russian-Jewish origin, Sonia Haft Greene.

Meanwhile, Lovecraft had become a fairly frequent contributor to *Weird Tales* and also earned a pittance by ghost writing and manuscript revision. But he never really earned his living expenses, frugal though these were. The modest legacy that he had inherited from his parents kept shrinking until, at his death, it was nearly all gone.

After a year in New York, during which Lovecraft tried to find a job with almost complete lack of success, his wife was compelled to accept work in Ohio. Lovecraft refused to go with her and spent another year in New York. Then, hating the metropolis with a frenzied hatred, he fled back to Providence and spent the rest of his life there, living with a pair of indulgent aunts. He and Sonia were more or less amicably divorced.

Lovecraft passed the rest of his life ghost writing, writing weird stories, and making bus tours of the United States and Canada. Little by little he gave up his ethnic prejudices, until at the end he was heartily ashamed of his earlier bigotry. He had also changed from a political ultra-conservative to a Socialist and New Dealer before he died of cancer at forty-six.

Lovecraft sold sixty-odd professionally published stories, all but a few of which appeared in *Weird Tales.* He had read all the earlier masters of fantasy but was most influenced by Poe, Dunsany, and Machen. Several of his earlier stories are patently Dunsanian.

Lovecraft is best remembered for about a dozen stories, mostly novelettes written in his later years, which developed the so-called "Cthulhu Mythos." In this fictional cosmogony, a hostile race of beings of supernatural powers, the Great Old Ones or the Ancient Ones, once ruled the earth but were subsequently defeated, banished, or restrained. Now and then, ignorant mortals tamper with the restraints upon the Ancient Ones, who thereupon begin to manifest themselves in terrifying fashion. The squid-headed Cthulhu, who sleeps at the bottom of the sea, is one of these powers.

Some of Lovecraft's stories are laid in his own New England; his "Arkham," where ghoulish things happen, is a thinly disguised doublet of Salem. Lovecraft borrowed ideas from Poe, Dunsany, Robert W. Chambers, and Ambrose Bierce. The fictitious book of deadly spells, *The Necronomicon,* which plays a part in several stories, was supposed to have been composed about A.D. 730 by a mad

Arabian poet, Abdul Alhazred. Lovecraft's scholarly quotations from and allusions to the book caused librarians and booksellers to be plagued by people inquiring after it.

Lovecraft suffered from literary faults, the worst being a prolix, adjectival style derived from Poe. A modern reader does not shudder because he has been repeatedly told that something is "horrible," "ghastly," or "blasphemous." Still, Lovecraft had an imagination of immense power, turned out much good, sound entertainment, and exercised wide influence.

Much of Lovecraft's influence was exerted through letters. He was a fantastic letter-writer; he is estimated to have written something like 100,000 letters. The time he spent on letters was one of the reasons for his perpetual poverty. Through his letter-writing, he collected a circle of friends and admirers, with whom he swapped fictional concepts. Some of these he recruited into amateur journalism, and their amateur periodicals became the first science-fiction fan magazines. Lovecraft, in fact, acted as a kind of midwife to the science-fiction fan movement, although he died just too soon to see its blossoming.

One of Lovecraft's pen pals and fellow *Weird Tales* writers was Clark Ashton Smith (1893-1961). Smith was born and spent nearly all his life at Auburn, in north-central California, where his parents engaged in chicken farming. In his youth, Smith considered himself primarily a poet and was, in fact, hailed as one of America's leading poets. By the standards of the time, his verse exhibited dazzling color and skill. But for the poetical revolution led by Pound, Eliot, and other devotees of free-form verse, Smith might still be deemed a leading American poet.

Smith became a writer for *Weird Tales* in the middle 1920s, but over half of his ninety-odd stories appeared in 1931-35, when he needed the money to support his aged parents in their dotage. After they died in 1935 and 1937, Smith went back to poetry and to drawing and rock carving, so that his stories appeared only at long intervals. He wrote conventional science fiction and supernatural horror, but his best-remembered stories are somewhat Dunsanian fantasies laid on imaginary continents of the past or future or on other worlds. The stories combine an elaborately euphuistic style, bedizened with rare words, a sardonic humor, and an uninhibited bent for the macabre. Nobody since Poe has so loved a well-rotted corpse.

Another member of the Lovecraftian circle was Robert Ervin Howard (1906-36) of Cross Plains, Texas. During his short life, Howard turned out a huge volume of general pulp literature: sport, detective, Western, historical, and oriental tales, besides his many contributions to *Weird Tales.* Some consider his best stories to have been his humorous Westerns.

Howard's most successful fictions, though, were the tales laid in an imaginary prehistoric world, existing between the sinking of Atlantis and the beginning of recorded history. Howard called this period the Hyborian Age and worked out a pseudo-history and a pseudo-geography for it. His Hyborian hero is Conan the Cimmerian, a gigantic barbarian adventurer. After gory encounters with foes both natural and supernatural, Conan becomes king of one of the Hyborian lands.

During his short life, Howard published eighteen Conan stories, from shorts to a book-length novel, and left several others unsold or unfinished. In the 1960s, the Conan saga, revised and added to by one of the present writers and a couple of his colleagues, became paperbacked best sellers.

Howard, however, never lived to see his triumph. He suffered from excessive devotion to his mother and, although a big, burly, athletic man like his heroes, from delusions of persecution. His relations with his mother constitute an extreme example of the Oedipus complex. He took to carrying a pistol against enemies, who probably did not exist. When his aged mother lay dying, he put a bullet through his head.

Another member of the circle was August W. Derleth (1909-71) of Sauk City, Wisconsin. Derleth, who looked like a blond gorilla and had a gently courteous manner, was a writer of prodigious energy and productivity. His more than sixty books include detective stories, regional novels, and fantasy. Besides contributing stories to the Cthulhu Mythos, he was co-founder of Arkham House, which he set up initially to publish the works of H. P. Lovecraft. Eventually, Arkham House published all of Lovecraft's stories in book form, as well as many of those of Blackwood, Clark Ashton Smith, and other leading fantasists.

Other frequent contributors to *Weird Tales* during the thirties included Robert Bloch, Seabury Quinn, and Manly Wade Wellman. Bloch is a tall, sardonic Milwaukeean who added to the Cthulhu Mythos, wrote regular science fiction, and for many years has been largely occupied with script writing in Hollywood. Wellman wrote a number of tales about a psychic detective of the John Silence type and finally became a professor in North Carolina.

Quinn was in private life, appropriately enough, in business related to undertaking. Although not himself a mortician, he sold undertaking equipment and edited a trade journal in that field. Once, when he was in New Orleans, his contacts there, wishing to show him the pleasures of the town, took him to a fancy bordello. There the girls—all faithful readers of *Weird Tales*—were so honored by his presence that they offered him one on the house. It is interesting to note that, despite the naked girls on the covers, *Weird Tales* was never a lewd or salacious magazine. Its contents were as sexually pure as even the puritanical Lovecraft could have wished.

In the late 1930s, several leading contributors to *Weird Tales* died, while others departed for writing of better-paying kinds. In 1938, the owners of the magazine sold it to another firm. Two years later, Wright's health worsened. His new employers fired him, and he soon died. As the magazine's new editor, they assigned Dorothy McIlwraith, a middle-aged Scotswoman, who had been editing *Short Stories,* in its day a leading competitor of *Adventure Magazine*. Although an experienced editor, Miss McIlwraith lacked Wright's touch with the fantastic. The magazine lost its attractive variety, struggled along, suffered from the competition of other fantasy magazines, and ceased publication in 1954.

☆ ☆ ☆

Weird Tales was not the only medium for the publication of fantasy, although during most of its life it was the only periodical outlet for short stories in the genre. The usual trickle of cloth-bound fantasy novels continued, such as James Stephens's rewritings of the sanguinary myths of Irish legend or the massive novels of the British civil servant Eric Rücker Eddison. Eddison (1882-1945) created a series of medieval, magic-fraught fantasy worlds, in which princes, warriors, and Vikinglike barbarians fight, love, and philosophize. The best-known and most successful of these was *The Worm Ouroboros* (1922), perhaps the greatest single novel of heroic fantasy.

During the 1920s, Thorne Smith brought out his hilarious, ribald farces on imaginative themes, such as the "Topper" stories of drunken and lecherous ghosts; *Turnabout,* which exchanges the souls of a man and his wife; and *The Stray Lamb,* whose hero is turned into animals of various kinds.

At the other extreme are the serious theological fantasies of Charles Williams and C. S. Lewis. Williams (1886-1945) was an editor for the Oxford University Press and the author of the non-fiction *Witchcraft* (1941), an excellent introduction to this subject. In addition, Williams wrote seven novels, all erudite, subtle, moralistic, weighty, slow-moving theological fantasies. *Shadows of Ecstasy* (1933) follows the spirit of a recently-dead girl and a world-conquering sorcerer. In *Many Dimensions* (1931), the Stone of Solomon works magic in modern London. In *The Place of the Lion* (1947), amateur theurgy causes the things of this world to merge back into their Platonic archetypes.

Clive Staples Lewis (1898-1963), a professor at Oxford, was the leading spirit in an intellectual discussion group, the Inklings. They met weekly, either in Lewis's rooms or in a pub, to argue and to read manuscripts to each other. The group also included Charles Williams and J. R. R. Tolkien.

Lewis wrote a number of novels, also theological fantasies. Seven were juvenile fairy tales of the Narnia series, wherein a group of children find themselves in a parallel world with witches, talking animals, and similar wonders. Although the series has enjoyed considerable popularity, it has also been criticized, we think justly, because Lewis beats the reader over the head with his religious convictions. The dominant being of Narnia, for instance, is a super-lion, who turns out to be another incarnation of Christ.

Lewis also wrote several adult imaginative novels, of which three form the Ransom or Perelandra trilogy. In *Out of the Silent Planet* (1943), evil scientist Weston sends the protagonist Ransom to Mars. There Ransom finds a beautiful world, where all life coöperates under the guidance of the planetary ruling spirit or Eldil. Weston follows and begins shooting the natives until this spirit stops him. Ransom learns that things are less harmonious on earth because our Eldil has become perverted or psychotic. This is Christianity with touches of Gnosticism and Neo-Platonism—which, to be sure, influenced early Christianity.

In *Perelandra* (1944), Ransom goes to Venus, a planet of vegetable islands floating in a world-wide ocean. Ransom meets the Venerian Eve, a beautiful green girl. Satan (the Terran Eldil), having possessed Weston's body, turns up and tempts the green girl by suggesting that she wear clothes.

Finally, *That Hideous Strength* (1946) takes place on earth. A gang of evil scientists tries to gain control of Britain by means of a National Institute of Co-ordinated Experiments, or N.I.C.E. Ransom leads a group opposing the N.I.C.E. The cast also includes the enchanter Merlin, the severed but living head of an evil scientist, and Horace Jules, the figurehead director of the N.I.C.E. This Jules, a pudgy little man who speaks Cockney and pontificates on things he knows nothing about, is a venomous caricature of H. G. Wells.

Although Lewis was an able and erudite novelist, the first two Ransom novels sag under the author's didacticism. His Mars and Venus, which have never known the Fall, are so pretty and perfect as to be insipid. Lewis also uses symbolic names for his characters, as writers did in the seventeenth and eighteenth centuries with their Squire Allworthys and Captain O'Triggers. Lewis's "Weston" stands for "Western" (modern industrial) culture. His villains are scientists, to whom he attributes such curious intentions as exterminating all unnecessary plant and animal life and all backward races of man. Thus one may say that he wrote anti-science fiction, as did Aldous Huxley and Ray Bradbury. Still, *That Hideous Strength* is a good, gripping piece of story-telling.

From 1939 to 1943, Street and Smith Publications brought out a fantasy companion magazine to *Astounding Stories,* called *Unknown* (later *Unknown Worlds*). This stimulated an outburst of fantasy stories, many of which later appeared as books. The paper shortage slew this magazine, but another market for fantasy opened up in 1949 with the launching of the still flourishing *Magazine of Fantasy and Science Fiction.* Other magazines specializing in fantasy appeared in the decades after the Second World War. Most lasted only a few issues, except for *Fantastic Stories,* which, with several changes of name, has been active from 1952 to the present.

On the whole, adult fantasy remains a minor genre of limited market. Writers enter it more for their own satisfaction than for monetary rewards, since (with exceptions like Tolkien's *Lord of the Rings* and the Conan stories) it has, by and large, rewarded its writers less liberally than has straight science fiction.

☆ ☆ ☆

In the second quarter of the twentieth century, the growing number of science-fiction magazines encouraged writers to turn their attention to this field of imaginative writing. When *Amazing Stories* started, for example, Gernsback had difficulty finding good material. In his first issues, therefore, he ran reprints of such older writers as Wells and Merritt.

Abraham Merritt (1884-1943) was a journalist, who edited Hearst's *American Weekly* from 1912 to his death. His hobbies included archaeology, witchcraft, and raising exotic plants containing rare drugs and poisons. His nine imaginative novels show strong imagination, vivid description, complex plots, and glacial slowness. He often used the lost-race theme. In *The Ship of Ishtar* (1926), often deemed his best, the scholar Kenton gets a model of an ancient galley. As he watches, he suddenly finds himself aboard the real ship, sailing in some extra-dimensional world of strange natural laws.

[37]

Amazing continued under Gernsback until he failed in 1928, when Teck Publications took over his magazine. Gernsback soon got back into business. In 1929, he started a group of magazines that included *Wonder Stories.* Early issues of *Wonder* featured European science-fiction novels translated from the French and German by a small, goateed, former featherweight pugilist, librarian, and journalist named Fletcher Pratt.

Like many publishers operating on a shoestring, Gernsback was lavish with promises that he often neglected to keep. Pratt sometimes coerced Gernsback into paying what he owed by threatening to quit in the middle of translating a serial, of which the first instalments had already appeared.

In 1930, Clayton Publications started *Astounding Stories.* Four magazines were then available: *Weird, Amazing, Wonder,* and *Astounding.* Of these, *Amazing* and *Astounding* have, with changes of name, survived.

During this time, several of the ablest imaginative writers were represented little or not at all in the new magazines but were being published in hard-cover books. Among these were Eric Temple Bell (1883-1960), a professor of mathematics at California Institute of Technology and one of the world's leading mathematicians. Besides his technical works and his popularizations of science and philosophy, Bell wrote a dozen science-fiction novels under the name of "John Taine."

Bell was a man of towering stature, with an eagle face surmounted by bushy gray hair and eyebrows and the burr of his native Aberdeen on his salty tongue. His stories usually start with a scientific anomaly or mystery. His people set out to investigate. The menace grows, and the tale ends in a violent natural upheaval. *The Forbidden Garden* deals with frightful mutations in the Himalayas. *The Greatest Adventure* discovers a swarm of monsters in the Antarctic, while in *The Iron Star,* a radioactive meteorite makes those exposed to it devolve back towards their simian ancestors.

Another successful writer was the British novelist S. Fowler Wright, who also wrote detective stories. Wright's sixteen imaginative novels are serious, intense works in a dry, precise style. Characters all speak the same stiff, formal English, and the story gets off to a very slow start. But, if a reader perseveres, the story becomes so absorbing that he cannot stop before the end. Wright's work is characterized by massive, powerful ideas, originality, tension, and many strong prejudices. A Rousellian primitivist, he was opposed to birth control and had only contempt for the lower classes. His scientists, like those of Lewis, were satanic creatures. In short, Wright was a kind of gloomy, aristocratic, anti-scientific Wells.

The Adventure of Wyndham Smith tells of a man whose soul is displaced into the body of a man of the far future, when mankind, bored with utopian perfection, has resolved to commit mass suicide. The novels *Deluge* and *Dawn* deal with a catastrophe that drowns most of the world's lands and raises others from the sea bottom. *The World Below,* Wright's most original work, takes its hero into the future, when life forms have evolved out of all resemblance to those of today. The descendants of men are 50-foot hairless giants, who live underground and war against a race of colossal insects from the other side of the earth.

In 1930 appeared *Last and First Men,* by William Olaf Stapledon, a lecturer at the University of Liverpool. This novel is one of the most cosmic forecasts ever attempted. It pursues men through eighteen different species, including flying men, giant brains, and a race of supermen with five eyes apiece, living on Neptune.

☆ ☆ ☆

The Depression of the 1930s bore hard upon the new magazines. In 1932, *Astounding* went bi-monthly and ceased the following year. It was bought and revived as a monthly by Street and Smith Publications under the editorship of F. Orlin Tremaine. In 1935, *Wonder Stories* underwent a similar crisis. It emerged as *Thrilling Wonder Stories,* edited by Mort Weisinger for the Standard Magazine—Better Publications combine. Then, in 1938, Ziff-Davis Publications of Chicago bought *Amazing* and placed it under the editorship of Raymond A. Palmer.

During the middle years of the decade, new writers arose.

Otto Binder, writing as "Eando Binder,"[8] published a series of stories in *Amazing* about a virtuous robot named Adam Link. Arthur J. Burks told in *Jason Sows Again* (*Astounding,* 1938) how the United States would win a war with an aggressive oriental empire by means of a machine that duplicates soldiers. A Briton, John Russell Fearn, contributed many tales of slam-bang action. A physician and psychiatrist, David H. Keller, published stories with a biological slant.

P. Schuyler Miller, of Schenectady, New York, an educator and an avid amateur archaeologist, exploited archaeological and anthropological themes. Nathan Schachner, a New York lawyer who wrote scholarly biographies and studies of medieval university life, composed a "Past, Present, and Future" series about an ancient Greek, a modern man, and a man of the future. In the remote future, this trio seeks a decent civilization in a world that has specialized to the point of insanity. A patent lawyer and engineer, Roger Sherman Hoar, as "Ralph Milne Farley," wrote time-travel stories and a series about his "radio man," who accidentally broadcasts himself to the planet Venus.

One of the nation's most prolific writers was William Fitzgerald Jenkins, born in Norfolk, Virginia, in 1896 and the author of well over a thousand stories. His writings include not only science fiction but also Westerns, detective stories, adventure stories, love stories, and comic-book continuity, as well as reports on scientific research, technical articles, and radio and television scripts. He was also an inventor. Most of his science fiction was written as "Murray Leinster," reserving "Will Jenkins" for writings of other kinds. His story "Sidewise in Time" (*Astounding,* June 1934) first popularized the alternate time-track theme.

Two other large-volume producers of science fiction at this time were Jack Williamson and Edmond Hamilton, who may be considered together since they were and are close friends and wrote in similar veins. Williamson—in maturity a tall, big-boned, rugged-looking man with a cowboy slouch, shy and taciturn with strangers—was born in 1908 in what was then Arizona Territory. He was reared in Mexico, in Texas, and finally in eastern New Mexico, where his family ran a cattle ranch. He began to write in the late 1920s and also to travel about the United States and Latin America. Some of his journeys were with Hamilton; once they guided a flatboat down the Mississippi to New Orleans, emulating Huckleberry Finn.

Williamson wrote space epics in the 1930s, such as *Legion of Space,* and sold to *Unknown* perhaps his most effective story, the werewolf novel *Darker Than You Think.* In later life, he became a professor at the University of Eastern New Mexico, where he still teaches courses in science fiction.

Hamilton, author of hundreds of imaginative tales as well as detective stories, was born in 1904 in Youngstown, Ohio, and spent most of his early life in that region. He held a variety of jobs and wrote science fiction when not traveling or cowpunching with his friend Williamson.

Hamilton wrote all but a few of the *Captain Future* novels, published by Standard Magazines in its periodicals throughout the 1940s. Their hero went about saving the solar system from doom with the help of a robot, an android, and a disembodied brain. Hamilton married a fellow writer, Leigh Brackett, herself an outstanding creator of space adventures.

Both Hamilton and Williamson wrote scores of stories in which the world was either saved or destroyed at the last minute. There were jokes about "World-saver Williamson and World-destroyer Hamilton," although the distinction between the two was not so sharp as the sobriquets imply. It was said that many of their stories could be summarized thus: Three men go out to save the world. One goes mad, one is eaten by the Things, and one returns to tell the tale.

In the late 1930s and early 40s, Henry Kuttner (1914-58) was for some years the most prolific single writer of imaginative fiction. This was not realized for several years because Kuttner used at least seventeen pseudonyms. He was extremely versatile, writing fantasy, humor, space epics, and stories of atomic doom with equal adroitness. His work ranged from mere pulp potboiling to stories of classic quality.

A small, dark, quiet man, Kuttner, for all his talent, suffered from excessive adaptability. Hence he tended to imitate whatever kind of tale happened to be fashionable in any year, and thus failed to develop a distinctive style of his own. He was one of H. P. Lovecraft's later correspondents and married another member of the Lovecraft circle, Catherine L. Moore.

C. L. Moore had made her reputation with a Martian story, "Shambleau" (*Weird Tales,* November 1933) and remained, until lured away into script-writing jobs in Hollywood, one of the most successful purveyors of intense emotion in the imaginative field. After she married Kuttner, practically all their work was done in collaboration. In 1950, the Kuttners went to college. Both obtained bachelors' degrees, and Kuttner was working on his master's degree when the heart trouble from which he had long suffered carried him off.

☆ ☆ ☆

From 1930 on, a young engineering graduate of Duke University, John W. Campbell (1910-71), sold many ingenious stories, including a series about a pair of interplanetary explorers named Penton and Blake. In 1937, Campbell replaced Tremaine as editor of *Astounding Stories,* the title of which he presently changed to *Astounding Science Fiction,* and later to *Analog.* He continued writing, mostly as "Don A. Stuart," until his employers insisted that he devote all his time to his magazines. Meanwhile he had composed a terrifying novel, *Who Goes There?* (*Astounding,* August 1938), about a hostile shape-changing entity in the Antarctic.

As the years went by, John Campbell became an enthusiastic apologist for many pseudo-scientific vagaries. Campbell had tried scientific research himself, found it uncongenial, and left it for fiction. We suspect that he cherished the thought that, although he was not destined to be a great and famous scientist, he might be the discoverer of such a person.

The first and most important of Campbell's "discoveries" was L. Ron Hubbard, the founder of Dianetics and, later of Scientology. Born in Nebraska in 1911, Hubbard was a tall, red-haired adventurer of overpowering personal charm, the scion of a naval family. After briefly attending George Washington University Engineering School, he led a picaresque life; singing on the radio, serving a hitch in the Marines, and organizing a cruise to the Caribbean.

Hubbard was an established writer of pulp fiction, especially of Western and sea stories, when he burst into science fiction in 1938. From then until 1942, he sold stories under his own name and also as "Rene Lafayette" and "Kurt von Rachen." He wrote some rollicking adventure-fantasy novels that fit into the modern classification of sword-and-sorcery and other, more serious, tales wherein the hero is a lonely, solitary, aristocratic natural leader who has to master the benighted clods for their own good.

After a sea-going career as an officer in the U.S. Naval Reserve during the Second World War, Hubbard returned to science-fiction writing. He was quoted as having said: "Some day I'll pull something that'll make Barnum look like a piker." He did.

In the May 1950, issue of *Astounding* appeared an article by Hubbard called "Dianetics, the Evolution of a Science." The article was followed by the book *Dianetics, the Modern Science of Mental Health,* which began with the claim: "The creation of dianetics is a milestone for Man comparable to his discovery of fire and superior to his invention of the wheel and the arch."

The book became a best seller despite the fact that medical men denounced it, and unsympathetic readers dismissed it as gobbledygook. Campbell was fascinated by Dianetics for over a year; then he broke with the movement. Hubbard went on to develop new doctrines involving reincarnation and the extraterrestrial origin of man, and at last emerged as leader of the Church of Scientology.[9]

Following his break with Hubbard, Campbell became in succession a propagandist for extrasensory perception, for a mental device called the Hieronymous machine, for an alleged "magnetic current," and for a perpetual-motion contraption called the Dean Drive.

Despite his interest in pseudo-scientific ideas, John W. Campbell built up a well-deserved reputation as the greatest science-fiction magazine editor of all time. He continued as editor of *Astounding—Analog* for thirty-four years, until his

[43]

sudden death. He was largely responsible for the marked rise in literary quality that took place in the writing of science fiction; for he demanded only the best. He had sound knowledge of literary techniques and actively coached his writers, criticizing their manuscripts in detail and giving them plot ideas to work on. Several leading science-fiction writers of the period following the Second World War served their apprenticeship under Campbell.

One such was Robert A. Heinlein. Born in Missouri in 1907, Heinlein graduated from the U.S. Naval Academy but was retired for physical disability in 1934, after two years of service. Following a try at silver mining and professional politics, he became a full-time writer and enjoyed a quick and lasting success. During the Second World War, he worked as an engineer for the U.S. Navy at the Naval Base in Philadelphia, along with Isaac Asimov and Sprague de Camp.

After the war, Heinlein went back to writing. He had already made his name with a series in *Astounding* built around a "future history," extrapolated from the present over the next 600 years. One of his later juvenile novels, *Rocket Ship Galileo,* became (after drastic alterations) the pioneering space motion picture, *Destination Moon,* on which Heinlein worked as a technical advisor.

Over the ensuing years, Heinlein has written many juvenile and adult science-fiction novels, some of which, like *Stranger in a Strange Land,* present radical sociological ideas. Among his finest works are the novel *The Moon Is a Harsh Mistress* and the short story "The Green Hills of Earth." Heinlein is noted for his skill in treating imaginative themes in a realistic, slice-of-life manner.

Another of Campbell's protégés was L. Sprague de Camp, co-author of the present book. Born in 1907 in New York City, de Camp was graduated from the California Institute of Technology with a degree in engineering and received his master's degree from Stevens Institute of Technology. His career as a science-fiction writer was interrupted by a term of service as an officer in the U.S. Naval Reserve during the Second World War; but at the end of the war, he settled in the Philadelphia area and has spent the past thirty-odd years as a free-lance writer.

Although de Camp has traveled widely and has devoted himself to historical and archaeological subjects, such as *The Ancient Engineers* and *Great Cities of the Ancient World,* he has never lost touch with the field of imaginative fiction. His early science-fiction novels *Lest Darkness Fall* and *Rogue Queen* are still in print and widely read. His contributions to the Conan saga are known to most readers of swordplay-and-sorcery stories. And his biography of H. P. Lovecraft pays tribute to an outstanding writer of tales of the imagination.

Also trained under John Campbell was Lester del Rey, who was born in 1915 in Minnesota of remotely Spanish descent and whose real name is Ramon Felipe San Juan Mario Silvo Enrico Alvarez-del Rey. His early experiences include working as a carnival hand, evangelist, lumberjack, and short-order cook and awaking one morning on a camping trip to discover, inside his sleeping bag, a coiled rattlesnake asleep on his chest. He lay without moving for several hours until the sun warmed the air and the serpent departed about its business.

A warm-hearted man with an air of gentle good nature, del Rey is one of the most astute and erudite of the writers of science fiction. Married to Judy-Lynn del Rey, science-fiction editor at Ballantine Books, he is now the fantasy editor for that company.

Del Rey has published several novels, of which the most memorable is *Nerves,* and has written over 100 science-fiction stories. He is a master of pathos. His most touching story is "Helen O'Loy," a science-fiction classic about a lovely, devoted robot who, serving as a maid, falls in love with and marries her owner.

Still another writer of Campbell's group was Isaac Asimov, born in 1920 in the Soviet Union and brought to the United States at the age of three. He grew up in Brooklyn, began writing fiction at twelve, and eventually wrote his way through Columbia University. Following the Second World War, in which he worked as a chemist for the Naval Air Material Center, he served a hitch in the Army, returned to Columbia, got a Ph.D. in chemistry, and taught biochemistry at Boston University. Evenings and weekends he wrote, and everything he wrote sold.

In his early writing years, the ebullient and lovable Asimov specialized in robot stories and developed the now famous "three laws of robotics." He composed a series about a future Galactic Empire and a "Foundation" that contends with it. These stories, like all his later tales, give evidence of his omnivorous reading and his eidetic memory.

Asimov's short story "Nightfall" is one of the greatest science-fiction stories ever written. His award-winning novel *The Gods Themselves* should not be missed by any reader in the field. In addition to his science-fiction tales, this versatile and energetic man has written on a wide variety of subjects, such as the two-volume work *The Intelligent Man's Guide to the Physical Sciences & The Intelligent Man's Guide to the Biological Sciences* (1960), and *Asimov's Guide to the Bible* (1968). At last count, the total number of Isaac Asimov's books was fast approaching two hundred. His admiring colleagues can only wonder how he does it.

☆ ☆ ☆

Science fiction grew in popularity in the years 1939-1941, and the number of magazines increased to over twenty. This expansion encouraged a host of new writers, many of whom, like Asimov and Heinlein, had scientific or technical training. These new writers brought to the genre not only a more realistic grasp of science and technology but also greater skill in portraying character and motivation than had been usual in pulp magazines of earlier times. Science fiction was coming of age.

Unfortunately, Pearl Harbor with its attendant shortages of publishers, writers, and paper brought about the collapse of this boom. *Astounding Science Fiction,* which had expanded from "pulp size" (6½" x 9") to "flat size" (8½" x 11½"), now shrank to "digest size" (5½" x 7¾"). *Unknown Worlds* vanished completely. Other magazines fell like autumn leaves until there were only nine. Britain's two imaginative magazines, *Tales of Wonder* and *Fantasy,* also disappeared.

With the end of the war, however, many discontinued

science-fiction magazines were revived and new ones were started, until by 1950 their number, once again, reached about twenty-five. The demand was never really large enough to support so many periodicals; consequently only between five and ten have survived to the present time.

Still, many new writers entered the magazine field during that period, bringing such varied talents as those of Alfred Bester, James Blish, Ray Bradbury, Arthur C. Clarke, "William Tenn" (Philip Klass), and Jack Vance.

The witty and worldly Arthur C. Clarke, an Englishman now living in Ceylon, an adventurer whose hobby was scuba diving and treasure-hunting amid ancient underwater wrecks, has become one of the foremost science-fiction writers living today. Besides his book of charming fantasies, *Tales of the White Hart*, he has written several memorable science-fiction novels, among them *Childhood's End* and the story that became the movie *2001*.

Many of this generation of science fiction writers found jobs waiting in the motion picture industry, as an increasing number of imaginative stories were turned into movies for the screen and television. Thanks to the versatility of modern camera work, places that never were and machines that never can be spring to life for the viewer.

☆ ☆ ☆

Between the two World Wars, paperbacked books were almost unknown in the United States, although they continued to flourish in Europe. They were revived in America during the Second World War because they used less paper and shipping space. Once widely accepted, paperbacked books so grew in popularity that publishing them became a major business. The publishers not only issued and reissued old science fiction, but also provided a growing market for new material, especially of novel length.

In the post-war years, paperbacked books largely replaced, as a source of popular reading matter, both the pulp and the slick magazines, such as the *Saturday Evening Post* and *Collier's*. The virtual disappearance of both pulps and slicks drastically shrank the market for the American short story. In fact, the few science-fiction magazines published today offer the main remaining market for this art form. Hence, in the imaginative field, the outlets for novels have grown at the expense of those for short stories and novelettes.

It is still a working principle that an established writer can easily sell a novel and, a bit less easily, a collection of his short stories. But, while an obscure writer can nearly always sell a good novel, he can rarely sell a short-story collection. Other things being equal, a novel is more likely to profit a publisher than is a short-story collection by the same writer. Failure to realize this fact was one of several reasons for H. P. Lovecraft's poverty and obscurity during his lifetime.

☆ ☆ ☆

For a decade after 1945, fantasy fared badly. With the demise in 1954 of *Weird Tales* and the failure of several would-be successors, it seemed as if fantasy had become a casualty of the Machine Age. Then came a surprising revival, especially of fantasy of the heroic or swordplay-and-sorcery type. This rebirth of fantasy began with the publication between 1954 and 1955 of the great three-volume novel, *The Lord of the Rings,* by J. R. R. Tolkien.

John Ronald Reuel Tolkien (1892-1971) was an Oxford professor and a close friend and fellow Inkling of C. S. Lewis. He had already achieved eminence as the author of a successful juvenile fairy tale, *The Hobbit* (1937). His new work, which may be considered either a three-volume novel or a set of three sequels, was a quest story of immense grandeur, vividness, and readability. Laid in a vaguely prehistoric age, it tells of the efforts of a band of human beings, Hobbits (pudgy small humanoids), Elves, and Dwarves to thwart the world-conquering designs of an evil being named Sauron.

The hard-cover books had a modest success in America and won somewhat more acclaim in their native United Kingdom. They aroused extreme critical reactions, both pro and contra, and gathered a cult of fanatical admirers. In the middle 1960s, *The Lord of the Rings* was reprinted in paperback and, to the delighted surprise of the author and publishers, became a runaway best seller. It proved especially popular with science-fiction fans and college students.

At the same time, Sprague de Camp persuaded a paperback house to reprint the Conan stories, with additions by himself and a couple of his colleagues, Björn Nyberg and Lin Carter. Thus revived long after Robert E. Howard's death, the Conan tales achieved a popularity in the field of heroic fantasy second only to Tolkien's *Lord of the Rings.* Perhaps readers had grown weary of the puny, miserable anti-heroes who had dominated fiction during the 1950s.

☆ ☆ ☆

After 1945, new trends also appeared in science fiction. Some writers drew so heavily on the science of psychology that for a while the stories in *Galaxy Science Fiction* were alluded to as "psychiatric fiction." Other writers adopted a sentimental or anti-scientific point of view. Ray Bradbury, who like several other eminent writers had started in *Weird Tales,* achieved great popularity with stories of this type. Although Bradbury makes little use of science and technology, he is such a master stylist that many of his stories are gems of mood and feeling.

In the 1960s, several younger writers sought to adapt to imaginative fiction the unconventional narrative techniques pioneered half a century earlier by the Irish writer James Joyce in his huge experimental novel *Ulysses* (1922). These methods included the stream of consciousness; the rapid shift of scene through time and space; the detailed, literal realism of the "slice-of-life" story; and the avoidance of the structured plot of the well-wrought tale. Some critics hailed these experimenters as the "New Wave" and called the older writers obsolete. Others denounced the New Wave as ruinous to imaginative fiction.

Foremost among the writers identified with the New Wave were J. G. Ballard, Samuel Delany, and Michael Moorcock. Several others like Brian Aldiss, Harlan Ellison, and Roger Zelazny are sometimes mentioned in this connection, although they have not always considered themselves New Wavers. It will be interesting to observe the directions along which their writing develops in future years.

Much has been said about the New Wave, pro and contra. While artistic experiments are desirable lest the arts stagnate, and while some artistic experiments produce lasting results, in the nature of things most experiments fail. Although some good New Wave stories have been written, many others give the impression that the author is trying, by stylistic eccentricities, to hide the fact that he does not have an interesting story to tell.

Bizarre methods of presenting a story have been encouraged in the 1970s by the rising interest in imaginative fiction among members of the academic profession. There has been an extraordinary growth of science-fiction courses in schools and colleges. Many teachers of these courses know little about science fiction since Jules Verne and H. G. Wells, because until quite recently the bug-eyed monster magazines and all the tales between their covers were considered "cheap pulp trash," unworthy of attention. Some modern writers seem to be angling for the approval of academe by using methods that have worked—or at least made a stir—in mainstream fiction. But a technique that is attuned to a professor's idea of "literature" may or may not please the buyers of science-fiction magazines and paperbacks; and it is on the approval of the latter that the writer's income ultimately depends.

We cannot now predict what effect the New Wave and similar movements will have on science-fiction writing in the future. It seems likely that some of the techniques introduced by present-day writers will prove useful—but only occasionally useful—in future stories in this genre.

After all, imaginative fiction is escape fiction. It is primarily designed for the entertainment of the reader. Thus it is important to most readers that the tale be well-wrought and that it stimulate their thinking, stir their emotions, and enrich the day-dreams that are for all of us the icing on the cake of life.

EDITORS AND PUBLISHERS

Socrates once chided his fellow-philosophers because they lectured for vulgar money. This, he said, would debase their philosophy. When Protagoras heard of his colleague's strictures, he remarked that he knew of no reason why philosophers did not have the same right to eat as other people.

The same applies to writers. We have therefore approached this book as commercial writers writing for other commercial writers. Dr. Samuel Johnson once said: "No man but a blockhead ever wrote except for money"; an extreme statement, perhaps, but still a useful corrective to airy-fairy estheticism.[1]

In 1942, one of the authors sat in the headquarters of the U.S. Navy in Manhattan, facing three officers gathered to interview him as to his fitness for a commission in the U.S. Naval Reserve. These men seemed interested in the fact that, on the questionnaires he gave his occupation as "writer." They had trouble, however, in putting their concern into words. After some beating about the bush, one said:

"What we want to know, Mr. de Camp, is: *Why* do you write?"

Sprague de Camp thought and answered: "To make a living."

They relaxed. We suppose they feared that he might say he wrote to express his soul or to convey his deathless message to the world. Not that there is anything wrong with expressing one's soul or conveying one's deathless message, provided that one has some other means of support. Still, most writers do have to consider the bread-and-butter aspect of their writings.

Before anyone can write for money, however, he must know about the people and institutions that have the money to pay for his words; that is, the book and magazine publishing companies and the radio, television, motion-picture, and comic-book industries.

When Sprague de Camp wrote the original *Science Fiction Handbook,* twenty-odd years ago, the science-fiction and fantasy magazines formed the major market for writings in this genre. There were about thirty magazines, most of them publishing science fiction only, a few publishing fantasy only, and a few publishing both. Most had circulations between 50,000 and 200,000 copies.

Since then, the magazine market has drastically shrunk. During the last decade, the number of magazines has varied from five to ten. Every few years, a new periodical is launched or an old one gives up its ghost. Most have been published monthly but a few bimonthly; going bimonthly eases the strain on a magazine in financial straits.

The magazines, however, are still important to the beginning writer of imaginative fiction, since they furnish the principal market for short stories. In the 1920s and 30s, the golden age of pulp magazines, the pulps and the slicks provided a gluttonous market for short stories. Now, however, nearly all the magazines in both categories have perished, leaving the science-fiction magazine as almost the last stand of the American short story. True, there are some other short-story markets, such as *Ellery Queen's Mystery Magazine,* the men's magazines, and a few women's periodicals, which publish occasional short stories. But the market for this particular art form is limited.

Almost all the existing imaginative magazines, at this writing, are published in "digest size" or 5¼" x 7½". Several attempts have been made in recent decades to launch imaginative-fiction magazines in other formats, but only one of these has endured. The existing magazines range in size from 130 to 178 pages, with an average of about 160. Of these, several pages are occupied by front matter (table of contents) and advertisements.

The remaining pages comprise an editorial, a book-review section, sometimes a group of letters to the editor, an occasional cartoon or poem, and a number (usually six to nine) of paid contributions. Of these, one is often an article, while the rest are short stories, novelettes, and sometimes an instalment of a novel being run as a serial. Making allowances for the space occupied by illustrations and by minor features, such as a prediction of the next issue, the number of paid words per issue averages around 65,000.

This is just about the length of the average detective story or a science-fiction novel. Book publishers view a novel of less than 50,000 words as rather short for their purposes. Exceptionally long novels run over 150,000 words; a few over 200,000; giant multi-volume works, like Tolkien's trilogy, *The Lord of the Rings,* well over half a million.[2] These facts are significant to the writer, because it does him no good to write a novel of 80,000 words, aimed at a magazine that buys nothing longer than 45,000 words.

Any story of less than 10,000 words is commonly classed as a short story; one of 10,000 to 20,000, as a novelette; one of 20,000 to 40,000, as a novella, and anything over 40,000 as a novel. Magazine editors have an inflationary tendency to use these names for stories below the lower limits listed here—for instance, calling a story of a mere 15,000 words a "novel," thus giving the newsstand buyer the impression that he is getting more than he really is.

Some magazines run serials, while others do not. A magazine that does may accept a story up to 100,000 words or even beyond. One that does not is unlikely to want anything over 45,000.

The question of magazine serials has long been debated. Many readers seem to want to eat their cake and have it, too. They object to serials but at the same time praise and remember good book-length stories. Their objection often seems to be less to the length of the story than to its being cut up into instalments. Younger readers, especially, do not like to wait between instalments and lack the self-control to save up the issues until they have the entire story in hand.

From the writer's point of view, a magazine's policy of publishing book-length stories is advantageous. There is a natural or optimum length for a story developed from a given idea. If the story is much longer than this, it will seem verbose and rambling. If it is much shorter, the reader will feel that the idea has not been fully developed or that important scenes or explanations have been skipped. In general, a story that deals with a big, massive idea involving elaborate assumptions should be longer than a story based upon a slighter idea. A story laid in an exotic setting requires length to develop this setting.

There are, therefore, many stories to which the writer cannot do justice in less than book length. Since it is to his advantage to sell a story not only for magazine publication but also later, as a book, and since this is hard to do with a story of less than 50,000 words, the writer will naturally favor a magazine that allows him his full length.

If, however, the only magazine interested in his book-length story has a length limit of 50,000 words or less, the writer must resort to one of several alternatives, none very satisfactory. He can write two versions of his story, one longer than the other. Sprague de Camp's novel *The Glory That Was* runs to 57,000 words in book form but was cut to 42,000 for magazine publication. Now, while there are few novels that would not benefit from some judicious cutting, so drastic a reduction is likely to impair the story. Or if the "natural" length of the story is the shorter one, the longer version may seem padded. When the difference between the two versions becomes as great as a 3/2 or a 2/1 ratio, the adaptation of the original version to such a different length becomes almost as much work as writing two different stories.

Alternatively, the author can write a series of novellas or novelettes in the 20,000 to 30,000 word range, about the same characters, in hope of splicing two or three such stories together to make one novel. Thus Pratt and de Camp combined their novellas "The Roaring Trumpet" and "The

Mathematics of Magic," first published in *Unknown,* to make *The Incomplete Enchanter.* The joints, however, are likely to show, so that the finished product is artistically less satisfying than a single, unified tale of book length.

The author can also write a number of independent short stories and novelettes, hoping that, when he accumulates enough good ones, he will find a book publisher for a collection of these tales. Many writers have done this. One must remember, however, that, other things being equal, a collection of short pieces by any one author is likely to sell fewer copies than a single long novel of the same wordage. From the publisher's point of view, such a collection seldom pays its way, unless the writer is one of the top men in his field. By and large, an established writer can sell either a novel or a collection of shorter stories; but although an unknown writer can usually sell a good novel, he may find himself unable to place a collection.

☆ ☆ ☆

Magazine editors like to compile a "balanced issue." A typical balanced issue might contain, say, one novella (or an instalment of a serial) of 20,000 words; one novelette of 15,000 words; five short stories averaging 5,000 words; and one article of 5,000 words; total: 65,000 words. For the 65,000 paid words comprising one issue of this magazine, the editor pays at a rate, depending on the length of the piece and the magazine's policy, of one to five cents a word. Some magazines pay more than others, and editors often pay more per word for shorter pieces than for longer. The writer can learn rates offered by a particular magazine, at a given time, by consulting the current *Writer's Market,* or the publications of the Science Fiction Writers of America, or by writing or telephoning the editor and asking him.

The rates given here are about twice what they were before the Second World War. While the rates have risen, they have not risen in proportion to the general rise in prices. These figures are good only for the time of the present writing (1975); continued inflation would doubtless elevate them further.

The lower limit of a given editor's rates is more important

to the writer, especially the new writer, than the upper. Most editors pay their lowest rate for most of the copy they buy, awarding the highest rate only now and then for exceptional stories or for stories by writers so well-known that they can command such rates. A writer who makes, say, a typical $150 on a short story and $1,500 on a novel is not likely to get rich just writing for the imaginative magazines.

Payment may be on acceptance of the story, or when the story is scheduled for publication, or on actual publication. Writers naturally prefer payment as soon as possible. The more prosperous the magazine, the sooner they are likely to get their money.

Editors vary as to just what rights they buy. A publisher purchases, at least, the right to print the story once in a magazine published in North America. This is called "first North American serial rights," and established writers often have this phrase made up into a rubber stamp and stamp it at the top of the first page of every piece they send to magazines. The magazine trade has the custom of using the term "serial rights" for "magazine rights," whether the story is run in one issue or is serialized.

The publisher may demand other rights, such as "first world serial rights," or "all serial rights" (which gives him exclusive control of all periodical publication, reprint as well as original), or "all serial and anthology rights," and so on up to "all rights."

It is to the author's advantage to limit the sale of rights as far as he can, so that he himself can sell the subsidiary rights as opportunity offers. If he writes a good story, he is likely to sell some anthology rights. Book-length novels in magazines are often later published in book form. Sales of radio, television, and motion-picture rights, while not common, occur often enough to make retention of such rights worth the author's while.

Authors have long disputed with publishers over such rights, and the writers' organizations have long campaigned to get magazine publishers to limit their purchases to first North American serial rights. A beginning writer, however, is not in a position to take a hard line with editors over rights. His best course is to submit his piece to an editor who pays high rates and to take rights into account and accept the best deal he can get. Publishers who demand many subsidiary rights are sometimes willing to return to the author, on request, a particular right for which the author has a buyer. Some publishers demand a share of the author's proceeds from such sales, although other publishers do not.

While we do not advise a writer to take a hyper-suspicious or belligerent attitude towards editors, he should not hesitate to ask the editor about the publisher's policies in matters of rates and rights. Once a story has been accepted, it is proper to try to bargain over subsidiary rights or other terms of the contract. The writer will do better at this if he knows what concessions that particular publisher is used to making.

☆ ☆ ☆

Like other men, editors of imaginative fiction come in all sizes, shapes, and temperaments. Because of the concentration of the publishing business in New York City, most of them are to be found in or near that city. Some used to edit magazines in different fields; others are former science-fiction writers who got tired of the uncertainty and low pay of free-lancing. Some are small cogs in big publishing machines, while others are large frogs in small puddles.

In a big publishing company, while one person has the official title of "editor" of a magazine, he is likely to have one or two assistants below him and a managing or executive editor above him. It takes at least two people to handle the reading, makeup, and correspondence connected with a single monthly magazine, not counting the art work, the printing, and the other minutiae of publishing.

Most editors work in small, glass-partitioned offices amid mountains of manuscripts, letters, galley proofs, proofs of covers and illustrations, back files of magazines, advance copies of next month's issue, a couple of typewriters, stationery, a pot of paste, scissors, ash trays, and the other clutter of the trade. They lead harassed lives, graphically described by the former science-fiction editor Samuel Mines:

Artist Snifflefritz, who has never seen a Martian

frommleglif in his life, has drawn a recognizable Terran salamander instead, and the picture has to be done over. It goes without saying that Snifflefritz cannot read, hence is unable to extract the description of a frommleglif from the story itself.

Who's going to do the illos for the new Crossen novel? Finlay stayed up all night finishing the work for the issue before last and he just got the stories for the last issue, so we can't throw this new batch at him with a three-day deadline. And we can't let anyone else do the lead pictures. . . .

Ye gods—the departments are ten days late! Do you want to go to press without 'em? . . .

Check this cover, willya? I can't find a scene in the story that looks anything like this!

There's a fan outside to see you. . . .

Listen, we can use a page of book reviews here in the back. Read four or five of these books—take an hour—and gimme about two columns right here. Sure, pick any four or five. There's only nineteen waiting to be read. . . .

Say, we still need three shorts and a novelet for the next ish. . . .

Look, did you see this? Two of these stories you got scheduled for this ish have practically the same plot. . . .

Can't we do something about the reading? There are stories from 1910 on the bottom of that pile. . . .

There's a fan outside to see you. . . .

Hey, you know you got BEMS[3] in practically every one of the illos for this issue? Damn thing looks like a zoo. . . .

Here's the fourth letter from this guy asking when the hell are we going to read his story. We bounced it two weeks ago . . . what's the matter with the mailroom? . . .

. . . for page eleven. Just whip up a nice little filler about the latest cosmotron at

Brookhaven. . . .

Take care of these releases for TV, will you?

There's a fan outside to see you. . .

. . . fan convention next month at Sauerbraten Tavern in East Liverwurst, N.J. Just make a short speech, answer questions from the floor, and bring along four or five Paul covers and some Finlay black and whites. . . .

. . . wish to write for your magazine. Kindly send full details as to the stories you use and how much you will pay me. . . .

We can't use that story you advertised last month . . . the novel ran way over-length. . . .

. . . can you tell me the pseudonyms of the following: Henry Kuttner, Robert Heinlein, van Vogt. . . .

This title is lousy. Got some quick brilliant suggestions for a new one? . . .

Hey, where are you going with my desk? To have it REPAINTED? NOW?

There's a fan outside to see you. . . .[4]

You can see why some editors come to their offices only one or two days a week and spend the rest of their working days at home, reading manuscripts without interruption. You can also see why an editor will not love you if you hang around his office, telling him the story of your life or engaging him in general chatter, or call him up for long, pointless telephone conversations. It is fine to telephone or call upon an editor when you have something definite to say or a legitimate question to ask. Before you do so, it would be well to write down a list of things to be said, say them briskly and concisely, note the answers, and go.

If, in a letter, you ask the editor a legitimate question, as about his policies or whether he likes an outline of a projected story, he will probably answer. If the missive is the usual letter-to-the-editor, commenting on the stories or arguing with the other correspondents in the letters section, he may print it in his readers' department if he has room in it and deems your letter interesting enough. Otherwise, he will discard the letter unanswered.

It is not that editors dislike letters of comment on the stories. They do, because such letters indicate how well their policies are working. Some run little box scores as departments in their magazines, listing the stories of a previous issue in the order of the letter-writers' preference. But editors cannot answer all these letters and edit their magazines, too.

It is asked: do editors read all the manuscripts they receive? That depends. Unless they are very hard up for manuscripts, they refuse to read manuscripts not in proper form. As John W. Campbell expressed it:

> Editors live by their eyes. They protect them, and flatly, absolutely refuse to read dim typing on gray paper. Believe it or not, some incredibly horrible offenses are committed against common sense—like the bird that sent in a neatly typed job, single spaced using red ribbon on yellow paper. He got it back almost instantly. Editors don't buy handwritten things, either; the linotypists refuse to have anything to do with it, and we don't see why an author should expect us to retype it to save him the trouble of learning his trade properly. Use a typewriter in the first place.

> Don't send a manuscript rolled; only a chimpanzee is equipped to hold one in reading position, and while he has the necessary four hands, he lacks critical judgment.[5]

Of the manuscripts in proper form, the editor will at least take a good look at all of them. He wants, he yearns for, stories of exceptional merit, and each new big manila envelope carries with it the promise that here at last is a new Asimov.

On the other hand, the editor does not read all manuscripts through. He knows from painful experience that a majority of the pieces will be from would-be writers—amateurs, tyros, non-professionals—and that, of these, most will be hopeless. After a little experience, he can detect stinkers by merely reading the first page or two, with a glance at a middle page and the last page to make sure that he is not missing something good. When asked what fraction of the stories they receive they actually buy, editors' estimates have ranged from one in ten to one in fifty.

Editors used to report on manuscripts—that is, inform the writers whether or not they meant to buy the stories—within two weeks of receiving the manuscripts. In recent decades, length of time in the editor's office has risen so much that many manuscripts are not reported on for eight or ten weeks. If the writer fails to hear from the editor within eight weeks of sending in his manuscript, he is well-advised to send the editor a query. There is a small but real chance that the manuscript has been mislaid, missent, or forgotten.

It goes without saying that a clear carbon copy or photocopy of every manuscript should be carefully filed before the original leaves the writer's possession, to protect the writer against possible loss of his manuscript.

Such a copy also, to some extent, protects the author against the fear of plagiarism, which troubles many beginning writers. Actually, the chances that the editor will steal some priceless idea from the manuscript, to use himself or to pass on to some crony, is negligible. Most manuscripts contain nothing worth stealing. So many thousands of stories have been published that, however original you think your idea, you could probably find an anticipation in print.

That brilliant idea of yours almost certainly comes from a common pool of ideas, built up over the centuries from the myths, legends, and stories of others. Bare ideas are not copyrightable and may be used by anybody. Copyright protects the particular use of words, sentences, and paragraphs to express these ideas. We are told that in the playwriting business, there is a danger of the theft of ideas, such as gags; but to worry about it in magazine publishing is a waste of time. On the very rare occasions when a work has been copied before publication, the author's possession of a dated carbon copy affords him the protection of common-law copyright.

If a story is too bad to be worth further discussion, the editor will probably return it with a printed rejection slip. If it is good, but not quite good enough for acceptance, the editor may write a letter explaining his rejection. Perhaps he will even suggest changes to make the piece more acceptable.

☆ ☆ ☆

It takes three or four months, and sometimes longer, from the time an editor buys the last story for a particular issue to the date that the issue appears on the stands. Art work takes a month; editing and makeup, another; printing, proof-reading, correcting, and binding another. A couple of weeks is then needed for wrapping, addressing, and mailing.

An editor may hold a purchased story for most of a year before printing it, because the earlier issues do not have a hole of just the right size for it. Sometimes an editor cuts or pads a story to make it fit. Since he works under pressure, he may cut out what the writer considers the most important sentence in the piece.

Being human, editors have prejudices, although they try to rise above them in choosing good stories. Their prejudices are likely to appear in their selection of marginal material, of which they always have plenty to choose from. John Campbell, for example, disliked any story that showed *Homo sapiens* as inferior to some extraterrestrial life form.

Authors do not ordinarily provide the pictures for their stories, save in the case where the author of a non-fiction article furnishes a sketch or a diagram to illustrate his piece. Usually, the publishing company's art department, if it has one, contracts with various artists. Only a few very versatile writer-artists have sold stories illustrated by themselves. On rare occasions, we have inclosed with the manuscript a sketch for the guidance of the artist in illustrating some technical point, such as the rigging of a ship, where the detail was important to the story.

☆ ☆ ☆

Imaginative novels have been appearing in book form throughout the past two centuries. With the growth of science fiction in the last fifty years, the number of such novels has increased to the point where several trade-book publishers have set up special science-fiction departments to handle them. Some lean especially towards science-fiction novels aimed at the adolescent trade. These differ from adult science fiction mainly in being held down to 50,000 words or less, with simple plots and no sex. The hero or heroine is usually an adolescent, too.

Many book publishers, large or small, are willing to consider good science-fiction novels. For information on this point, the current issue of *Writer's Market* is the best source. In addition, there are several small, specialist houses, similar to Arkham House. Sometimes they are called "semi-professional" publishers, because they are one-man operations, where the editor and publisher has another occupation and works on his publishing in off hours. In the last few years, several such ventures have appeared and are active at this writing.

Before you mail the manuscript of an entire book to any publisher, it is wise to write the editor, describing the book, stating its length, type, and age level, and outlining its plot and setting. The "slush pile" of unsolicited manuscripts has become so great that many publishers refuse even to look at unsolicited manuscripts. Once an editor asks to see the manuscript so described, you are off to a much better start and, moreover, have saved time, wear and tear on the manuscript, and postage. Unless the writer is very well-established, a self-addressed stamped envelope, with adequate postage, should accompany submissions of manuscripts.

Some large publishers care little whether a story has previously appeared in a magazine. Others prefer original manuscripts but will publish stories that have previously appeared. Authors are reluctant to sacrifice a magazine sale, when they can get it, for a book sale, which may be no more profitable and which can probably be made sooner or later anyway.

The small, specialist publishers, however, much prefer previously unpublished works. They do business largely by mail order with hard-core science-fiction fans, most of whom will have already read a story in its magazine form.

Previous magazine publication may not interfere with book publication, whereas previous book publication will greatly lessen the chance of later magazine publication. A writer, therefore, should make his arrangements for a magazine sale, if any, before undertaking a book sale. When you have either placed your story in a magazine or decided against doing so, it is time to undertake a book sale.

In selling to a book publisher, it is usually wise to start with the large book publishers, since they offer the widest distribution and usually the largest advances. If these all turn down the piece, you work your way down through the medium-sized to the small publishers. It is not too hard to sell a good science-fiction novel, especially if the story has not appeared in any magazine. Some of the little publishers, however, have been very slow in paying their authors, and others have quietly gone out of business owing their authors substantial sums.

The publisher (unless he is too small or too poor to do so) pays the author an advance against royalties. These advances run $1,500 and up for large publishers and $100 and up for the small specialists. Thus, to take some fairly typical present-day figures, if a book is priced at $7.50, and the publisher pays the author an advance of $3,000, the publisher must sell 4,000 copies before the book "earns out," as the phrase is, and the publisher begins paying the author royalties over and above the advance.

The publishing business has never been lavishly profitable, and the economic changes of recent decades have forced publishers to work on closer margins than ever and to sell larger numbers of copies of each title in order to break even on the cost of manufacture. Whereas a small publisher, having a lower overhead, may pay off his manufacturing costs with a sale of 2,000 copies, a large publisher is likely to have to sell at least 5,000 to achieve the same goal. In practice, therefore, most of the novels put out by large publishers do not pay for themselves, at least in their original form.

Then how, you may ask, do publishers make any money? Some do not, practically speaking, make money directly from retail book sales. But they stay in business by bringing out one successful book, which pays the deficits on several unsuccessful ones. They also collect a share of the sale of subsidiary rights: reprint rights, especially to book clubs and paperbacks; radio, television, and motion-picture rights;

foreign rights, and so on.

That is why publishers' contracts have clauses giving them a share of the income from the sale of such rights. When a publisher is in a good bargaining position, he will probably claim half of all such income. The writer, however, may be able to shave the publisher's share by hard bargaining, especially if he is dealing with one of the smaller publishers. We shall discuss the matter further in a later chapter.

☆ ☆ ☆

The great publishing phenomenon of the decade following the Second World War was the growth of the American paper-bound book business. At first, paperback publishers merely reprinted fiction that had already appeared in cloth-bound books, since at that time they did not have the editorial staff needed to read, judge, and edit original manuscripts. Since then, many such publishers have gone into the business of publishing original materials. At present, about a dozen such companies are active markets for imaginative fiction.

To get an idea of their relative size, one can consult *Writer's Market,* which lists the number of titles published by a publisher during the previous year. This is not, however, a sure indication of the financial condition of a company. A few years ago, Lancer Books was fourth, in number of titles published in a year, among publishers of science-fiction paperbacks. Soon afterwards, however, Lancer went into the kind of limited bankruptcy technically called "an arrangement under Title XI of the Federal Bankruptcy Act." In recent years, many publishing companies have merged with others or have become parts of conglomerates also controlling businesses of other kinds. Thus Random House now owns Ballantine Books, while the Italian Fiat Corporation has bought control of Bantam Books.

Paperback publishers may specialize either in trade paperbacks or in mass-market paperbacks. Trade-paperback publishers sell mainly through book stores. Their books are in a sense intermediate between mass-market paperbacks and cloth-bound books. They cost more than the former and have smaller sales, although they cost less than the equivalent cloth-bound books. Trade paperbacks run mostly to non-fiction and to reprints of older or "classic" works of fiction.

Mass-market paperback publishers, which publish most of the paperbacks of contemporary imaginative fiction, sell their products in great numbers, mainly through magazine outlets, such as drug stores and newsstands. Some paperback book shops carry paperbacks of both kinds.

A novel that has had a good run as a cloth-bound book has an excellent chance of being reprinted by a mass-market paperback publisher, but reprinting in a cloth binding of a book previously published as a paperback is much less likely. Some contracts provide for the simultaneous publication of a novel in cloth and in paper.

Publishers of cloth-bound books and trade paperbacks usually demand 50% of the money from a later mass-market paperback sale of a given book, although some established authors have been known to receive 60%. Thus an author may actually make less by selling to a cloth-bound book publisher and later to a paperback publisher than he would by selling to a paperback publisher in the first place.

On the other hand, publication in cloth has the advantage (aside from questions of prestige) that the book may be reviewed by many publications that do not usually review paperbacks, such as *Publishers Weekly, Library Journal,* the quality magazines, and the book-review sections of newspapers. Such reviews, if favorable, stimulate a larger total sale than the author could otherwise hope for. Few periodicals, outside the imaginative magazines and the fan publications, review paperbacks.

☆ ☆ ☆

Comic-strip continuity writing is a salaried occupation. One who works in this field should have no inhibitions about using old, worn-out, corny ideas. Some old-timers among science-fiction writers have gone into this line of work and made a living.

Comic books are one thing; syndicated comic strips in newspapers quite another. Comic books provide only modest salaries. A typical feature in such a publication is created by a team, consisting of a continuity writer and an artist. Under the supervision of the editor, the writer and the artist pass outlines, sketches, and dialogue back and forth until the finished strip emerges.

Newspaper comic strips are distributed by a small number of syndicates. This field is much more lucrative to the cartoonists and writers than comic books but is very hard to break into. Thousands of new strips are offered to the syndicates each year for every one that is sold.

The foregoing is the best information that we can give you about the present state of the publishing of imaginative fiction. What we have said on these matters will not remain accurate for more than a few years. So please check on our statements at every opportunity. The easiest way to find out about an editor's plans and policies is simply to ask him. The best way to get an over-all picture of the current needs and tabus of the various markets for imaginative fiction is to study, in the nearest public library, the latest editions of such writers' guides as *Writer's Market, The Writer's Handbook,* and *Literary Market Place,* and such periodicals as *Publishers Weekly* and the leading science-fiction and fantasy magazines.

READERS AND WRITERS

Years ago, when we had but lately been married, Catherine invited a couple to our apartment for dinner, and Sprague laid himself out to be pleasant to his bride's friends. While the women were busy in the kitchen, he showed the man some recent magazines containing his stories. The man glanced through a copy and asked:

"Do people actually *read* this stuff?"

Somebody must; but who? Before World War II, Campbell ran a questionnaire in *Astounding*. Among other things, he asked the readers to state their ages and occupations. About a third of those who replied were students. Another third held a wide assortment of jobs. The remaining third were scientists, engineers, and other technical persons. One of these last explained that he read the magazine because "in the stories, the experiments always work!"

In 1949, Campbell made another survey. The occupations reported were: engineering, 14.7%; mechanical engineering, 7.6%; sales and advertising, 7.5%; research, 7.3%; chemistry, 5.2%; professional (law, medicine, &c.), 5.2%; executive management, 5.0%; technicians (radio, radar, electronics, metallurgy, &c.), 4.5%; clerical and secretarial, 4.5%; auditing and accounting, 4.0%; armed forces, 3.5%; writers and editors, 3.3%; supervisory, 2.2%; architecture and design, 1.7%; civil service, 1.5%; agricultural, 1.2%; and smaller numbers in many other occupations. The readers were 93.3% male, but this time the students were not distinguished from

[69]

self-supporting adults. The average reader was just under thirty and a college graduate.[1]

Because of its bent towards science fiction in the pure or Gernsbackian sense and its high literary quality, *Astounding* was especially attractive to professional scientists. In the 1940s, the drug store at the Oak Ridge atomic center regularly sold over 150 copies within three days of receiving each issue.

Readers of imaginative fiction, for some reason, seem to be more self-conscious, vocal, and gregarious about their favorite literature than readers in general. While most of them quietly buy and read their favorite magazines, as do other readers, a minority of several thousand make an active, organized hobby of imaginative fiction. These are the fans. They write letters to the magazines; they belong to fan clubs; they publish their own amateur magazines; they hold conferences and conventions. When not engaged in fannish activity, however, they make their livings in as many different ways as readers in general.

Science-fiction clubs began early in this century. About 1923, Frank Belknap Long, later a leading imaginative writer but then a beginner, and two friends formed the habit of meeting weekly to talk about their interests, which were largely literary. When H. P. Lovecraft moved to New York, early in 1924, he was soon enrolled in the group, which eventually counted about a dozen members. They met, usually on Wednesday nights, sometimes at Long's apartment, sometimes at the Chelsea Bookshop, and sometimes at other members' apartments.

Noticing that the names of all the original members began with *K, L,* or *M,* someone suggested calling the group the Kalem Club. Along with the discussions of art, literature, and esthetics, literary members often read aloud their manuscripts. Such loosely organized discussion groups of intellectuals have flourished wherever numbers of such people were to be found, as in many large cities and university towns. Thus in the 1930s, three leading British fantasy writers—C. S. Lewis, J. R. R. Tolkien, and Charles Williams—belonged to the Inklings at Oxford. Because of the

Kalem Club's special orientation towards fantastic and imaginative fiction, it may be considered the first science-fiction fan society.

The Kalem Club was largely held together by the personal charm and magnetism of H. P. Lovecraft, and it became inactive soon after he returned to Providence in 1926. Other fan organizations, however, came into being in the late 1920s, when writers of letters to *Amazing Stories* began writing each other. Thus Jerome Siegel and Joseph Schuster, later the creators of the "Superman" comic strip, became acquainted and issued one of the first fan magazines: *Cosmic Stories*. About 1930, a circle of such correspondents had grown up among such enthusiasts as Ray Palmer, Jack Williamson, and P. Schuyler Miller, who formed a Science Correspondence Club. This took the pretentious title of the International Scientific Association and issued a fan magazine, *The Comet,* which appeared until 1933.

At the same time, a group called the Scienceers sprang up in New York. Members included Julius Schwartz, Julius Unger, and Mort Weisinger, all of whom became professionals. One member, Allen Glasser, called on Hugo Gernsback, who had awarded him a prize for an essay on the popularization of science fiction. Glasser informed his club that Gernsback had arranged for them to be addressed by a group of authors at the American Museum of Natural History. Speakers included a well-known engineer, G. Edward Pendray, a founder of the American Rocket Society, who had sold a few science-fiction stories. The members were in ecstasy until the Museum presented them with a bill for the use of the room, whereupon the club broke up amid recriminations.

During the early 1930s, other groups sprang up, split, fought, merged, and dissolved like protozoa under a microscope. There were disputes between adherents of "hard" science fiction and those of fantasy. There was a long quarrel between those who wished fan clubs to perform amateur scientific experiments and those who preferred the purely literary aspect of imaginative fiction. Such authors as Keller, Lovecraft, and Merritt helped and encouraged the fans by contributing to their publications. From this nucleus developed the booming fan movement of today.

The oldest fan club yet surviving is the Los Angeles Science Fantasy Society, active since 1934. Next in age comes the Philadelphia Science Fiction Society, formed in 1935 by a group that included Robert Madle, Milton A. Rothman, and Oswald Train. Other such groups exist in most of the nation's larger cities and in several foreign countries. If the reader wishes to get in touch with fan groups, writers or editors in the field can refer him to one or more such clubs in his vicinity.

Fan clubs meet weekly, bi-weekly, or monthly, sometimes in the quarters of members and sometimes in a rented room. Some are mere coteries of fellow enthusiasts; others have constitutions, officers, committees, and programs. A program may be a general discussion, or a paper delivered by a member, or a talk by a professional writer or editor. Some devotees of one particular writer, such as Burroughs, Howard, Lovecraft, or Tolkien, form clubs of their own.

Every year, fans arrange larger gatherings. There are a number of regional conferences, such as that in the late autumn in Philadelphia and that in Washington in the spring. A four-day world convention is held each year in a different city (and from time to time in a foreign country), usually on Labor Day week end. It draws thousands of fans, who listen to speeches and panel discussions, take part in auctions of books, rare magazines, and works of art, view dramatic performances and movies, compete for prizes at a costume party, attend a banquet and numerous private parties, renew old acquaintances and strike up new ones, and pursue the professionals with questions and requests for autographs.

Many clubs and individual fans issue amateur magazines, or fanzines, in a bewildering variety of formats: printed post cards, mimeographed sheets, and stapled magazines up to 150 pages long. They are printed by mimeograph, photo-offset, and even set type. They appear irregularly under such titles as *Anduril, ERBdom, Fantasiae, Laughing Osiris, Nebula, Nyctalops, Whispers,* and *Zymurgy.* Four of the oldest, still in continuous publication at this writing, are *Amra* (specializing in heroic fantasy); *Locus* (a newsletter of imaginative fiction, carrying information of interest to readers and professional writers); *LUNA Monthly* (book reviews and general information); and *Yandro* (general science-fictional comment).

For each copy, the fan publisher may ask from ten cents to $1.50 from fellow fans, or he may trade his publication for theirs, or give copies in return for letters and other contributions. Fanzines contain professional news and gossip, critical articles on various aspects of imaginative fiction, editorials, verse, and stories. The stories are mostly written by fans who hope to become professionals. Fan publishers urge professional writers and editors to submit articles for their magazines or to contribute stories gratis from their reject files. Some of this does a professional no harm, but he should beware of allowing such unpaid work seriously to cut into his regular working time.

Within the last year, at least eighty-odd fanzine titles have been published, including a number from foreign countries. The total number of titles that have appeared (and, usually, disappeared) in the last quarter-century must run into many hundreds. That these publications should prove as ephemeral as may-flies is not surprising. The publishers are amateurs, mostly young, who still have enough free time to lavish on their hobby.

Because many science-fiction fans are adolescents, and because some adolescents are given to exhibitionism and gaucherie, fans as a group have sometimes been scorned as eccentric. Actually, the average fan displays high intelligence, a voracious appetite for reading, and a personality type that often finds it hard to get along with ordinary people. The fans' interest in speculative literature gives them a common bond, which they do not often feel towards the average person.

Any group united by a literary or intellectual interest is a small minority *ipso facto*. Fans are no more eccentric than any other enthusiasts. At least, they never stand in line all night in the rain, as sports fans do, waiting for a ticket office to open in the morning.

☆ ☆ ☆

At gatherings, people have asked: "Mr. de Camp, do you think that I, too, should become a writer?"

Strictly speaking, the right answer to such a question is "No." Unless a person has so strong an urge that he will struggle to become a writer no matter what anybody says—if there is any doubt in his mind—he had better avoid this profession. He will almost certainly do better financially in some other occupation for which his physique, education, and personality qualify him.

What sort of people do become writers? There is no simple answer, because writers vary almost as much as people at large. In general, they are articulate persons with active, fruitful, imaginative minds—folk whose "brains they teem with endless schemes," and who can put their ideas into words without undue hesitation. One who hates to write letters and seldom does is probably not cut out to be a professional writer, although it does not follow that a voluminous correspondent is necessarily a potential fictioneer.

A writer must be intelligent—not necessarily a genius, but well up the intelligence scale. One below the average (that is, with an IQ of 100 or less) is wasting his time if he tries to make a living by writing.

A writer must be energetic and self-disciplined. A free-lance writer is his own boss. Unless he naturally drives himself harder than any other boss, he will not make a living. One who says: "I don't feel like working today; I think I'll golf or fish instead" will feel less and less like writing until he is loafing—and starving—all the time. Lazy writers tend to lead a hand-to-mouth existence, undergo painful domestic upheavals, and usually end up at some small, salaried job.

A writer must have a psychological toughness and resilience, so that, although time and again felled by frustration and disappointment, he promptly bounces back. If adversity, such as working for a year on a book and then having the publisher go bankrupt, throws a writer into such a fit of despondency that he cannot work at all, he is too sensitive for the rough-and-tumble of free-lancing. Disappointment is the daily lot of the self-employed writer. It seems even worse than it is, because a piece may be rejected twenty times before it is accepted. Hence, one eventual success entails twenty preliminary failures.

"Must you be a little crazy to be a writer?"

We could answer, no, but it helps. What such a question really means is: are writers more neurotic than most people?

There is no exact answer. Practically everybody is at least a little neurotic in one way or another. The perfectly normal person is a statistical abstraction. If he exists at all, we are sure that he is a very dull fellow. Possibly writers are slightly more neurotic than the average, although not to the point where they make themselves and those about them unhappy or die mad like poor Poe. If they were not a little aberrant or maladjusted, they would probably not become writers.

Writers vary much like people of other occupations. Some are extraverts and some introverts; some are conventional and others eccentric; some sober and others irresponsible. If they have any common characteristic besides their intelligence and word-mindedness, they probably tend towards the introverted type called the schizoid personality. Many started out as precociously intellectual but under-muscled children, bullied by their peers. Contrary to a common impression, writers are not necessarily fascinating companions, or staunch and helpful friends, or promising matrimonial material. They have a rather high suicide rate.

Neither are they necessarily acute observers. Careful observation, while always useful, is a requirement of the journalist rather than of the free-lance writer. A writer, however, must not be too unobservant and wrapped up in his own thoughts, or his writing will have so little touch with reality that it merely baffles his readers.

☆ ☆ ☆

When the first *Science Fiction Handbook* was written, the author listed eighteen of the then leading science-fiction writers, sent them questionnaires, and tabulated the results. The writers were Isaac Asimov, Leigh Brackett, Ray Bradbury, Edmond Hamilton, Robert A. Heinlein, Will F. Jenkins, Henry Kuttner, Fritz Leiber, Frank Belknap Long,

C. L. Moore, Eric Frank Russell, Clifford D. Simak, E. E. Smith, George O. Smith, Theodore Sturgeon, A. E. van Vogt, Robert Moore Williams, and Jack Williamson. A similar list made out today would naturally differ, but the results of the survey would be similar.

Two of the eighteen were women, both wives of men on the list. Of the eighteen, one was British, two naturalized Americans, and the remaining fifteen native-born Americans. Ages ranged from thirty-three to sixty-three, with an average of forty-four. In education, they had two doctors' degrees and four bachelors' degrees; several more obtained degrees, bachelor or advanced, after the time of the survey. Nearly all the rest had completed high school; six had had some college training without, at that time, having graduated from college.

Eight of the eighteen had a scientific background; they held degrees in science or engineering, or had done technical work like radio engineering, or both. Four had served in the Second World War and one in the First. Three others had military service or commissions without having served in either war, because they were more useful to the Government in their scientific capacities.

All but one had been married, and he was wedded later. Four had been divorced. One of these was between spouses, while the other three were living with second or third wives. Thirteen had their original mates—a record comparing favorably with the whole population. Nine had children of their own; two of these also had grandchildren. One had no children of his own but two step-children and a step-grandchild.

Nine of the eighteen—half—were full-time writers, although most of them also wrote in fields other than imaginative fiction. With one, imaginative fiction accounted for only a fraction of his total output. Of the other nine, four had scientific or engineering jobs, and four had jobs connected with publishing.

Answers to questions about working hours were vague and scattered. Many kept no track of time spent; and, even among those who answered, the details reported were different. How should one count time spent hoeing the garden while plotting a story? Four full-time writers estimated writing time from 30 to 115 hours a week, with an average of 54. Part-time writers' estimates ranged from 5 to 84 hours a week, with an average of 35.

For annual wordage of final-draft copy, the full-timers estimated from 70,000 to 350,000 words, with an average of 170,000. The part-timers gave respective figures of 70,000 to 250,000, with an average of 123,000. Full-time writers turned out more words per year, but not in proportion to the greater time they spent. Nearly all of these sold virtually everything they wrote—over 95%, anyway—and most of their few rejects found eventual markets.

Among their hobbies and avocations, they mentioned figure skating, fishing, guitar playing, natural history, painting, photography, tennis, and tinkering with machinery. Most added that they no longer had much time to pursue these hobbies. Clifford Simak stated: "My interests include chess, stamp collecting, and rose growing, but I'm a mediocre chess player, have virtually given up stamps through lack of time, have decided you can't grow roses in the villainous Minnesota climate. Most of my spare time is spent at reading."

The writers said that they read from 25 to 300 books a year, with an average of 125. Among writers who had influenced them, they named the following more than once: L. Frank Baum, Edgar Rice Burroughs, John W. Campbell (as an editor rather than as a writer), Lewis Carroll, H. Rider Haggard, Robert A. Heinlein, Rudyard Kipling, A. Merritt, Edgar Allan Poe, Jules Verne, and H. G. Wells.

PREPARING

FOR A SCIENCE-FICTION CAREER

Can one learn to write, or is it something inborn, genetic, or glandular, which no amount of teaching will improve? Yes and no. The ability to write is a blend of two components, *both* absolutely necessary. These are talent and technique. Talent is native and inborn, and we know of no way to put it into a head that lacks it. A person can be quite intelligent in other ways and still completely lack literary talent.

Writing technique, on the other hand, certainly can be learned, just as one can learn any other skill. In fact, it is not inborn at all; hence it must be learned. Other professionals, such as lawyers and physicians, spend years in special training before they are competent to practice. Why should a writer expect to master his profession any sooner?

If anything, technique or craftsmanship is more important in imaginative fiction than in writing of other kinds. In realistic fiction, especially that laid in a familiar setting, the writer can take it for granted that the reader knows about this milieu and the laws by which it runs. Everyone knows what an automobile looks like, what life insurance is, and how human beings reproduce their kind. In an imaginative story, on the other hand, the very assumptions differ from those of everyday life. The differences may be small or large; the setting may be utterly unfamiliar. Its appearance, institutions, laws, and customs must be brought home to the reader without letting the story bog down in description and

[79]

explanation. Every important exotic element of the story must be skillfully worked in.

☆ ☆ ☆

It is surprising how many people try to write commercially without knowing how to write English. The late Matthew Phipps Shiel never did learn. So, although he was a prolific writer of imaginative fiction for three decades (1895-1925) and although he had a powerful imagination, his works never achieved the recognition, at least in America, to which his ideas would otherwise have entitled him. His powerful fancies were expressed in an almost unreadable style, with endless, tortuous sentences, erratically punctuated. Here, from his best-known work, is an example:

> "Any tyro in psychical science will now sit and discourse about the reporting powers of the mind in the trance-state—a fact which Psychical Research only after endless investigations admits to be scientific, but known to every old crone in the Middle Ages; but I say that Miss Wilson's powers were *'remarkable,'* because I believe that, *in general*, the powers manifest themselves more particularly with regard to space, as distinct from time, the spirit roaming in the present, travelling over a plain; but Miss Wilson's gift was special in this, that she travelled all ways, and easily in all but one, east, west, up, down, in the past, the present, and the future."[1]

Knowing how to write means knowing English grammar, spelling, and punctuation; having an adequate vocabulary; and being familiar with the rules of composition. A person who tries to write without this knowledge is like a carpenter whose tools are dull, broken, or missing altogether.

We have seen copy submitted to a publisher by a writer who had evidently never heard of a question mark. When one of us taught a class of college freshmen some years ago, he found that many of his students did not know that a sentence is supposed to begin with a capital letter and end with a period. If you see nothing wrong with such sentences as "He stared like he had seen a ghost," or "An individual can return to any period of his entire life providing his passage is not blocked by engrams," you do not know enough about writing English to tackle fiction.[2]

It does not follow that a writer always obeys the rules. In theory, an infinitive is never split, but in practice some sentences can be made plain only by splitting an infinitive. There is, or was, a rule against using a preposition to end a sentence *with*. This rule, however, is merely an arbitrary tabu invented by eighteenth-century grammarians on the analogy of Latin. Shakespeare never heard of the rule. He wrote: ". . .and flee to others that we know not *of*." Moreover, if your narrator or speaker is uneducated, he should use the sort of English as such a person would use.

You should so well know the rules about infinitives and prepositions, and such alternatives as shall-will and who-whom, that you never need think twice about them. Moreover, you should know which rules may, can, or should be broken, and when. You should know not only standard English but such regional and class dialects as you may have occasion to use. To learn about such things, there are plenty of books, such as H. L. Mencken's *The American Language,* the files of learned quarterlies like *Dialect Notes* and *American Speech,* and dictionaries of slang and dialects.

It is good to keep your ears open, especially when traveling, to hear how people really speak. It does not follow that you ought to reproduce real speech exactly, or indicate odd pronunciations by respelling words phonetically. We shall, however, come back to this subject.

Would-be writers sometimes complain: "I took a course in English (or story-writing or journalism) but got nothing out of it." This is a bad sign. Not all courses are equally valuable, but if a writer has an eager, prehensile mind, he should get something out of any course, no matter how dim.

Although you can learn much from books and courses, it is an old and sound rule of magazine writing that your best textbook is a copy of the magazine for which you intend to write. Only an idiot would say: "I think I'll make some quick money by writing stories for the science-fiction magazines. Which one? Heavens, I don't know! I never read junk like that."

Beginning writers sometimes gain experience by attending writers' conferences. These affairs are mis-named, since they are not so much occasions where writers confer as where writers give informal classes to would-be writers on various aspects of writing. A typical conference includes a banquet with speakers, evening lectures by writers, editors, and agents, and "workshops" or courses in the novel, the short story, article-writing, agents and contracts, humor, imaginative fiction, verse, and similar subjects. The courses include talks and the analysis of manuscripts submitted by conferees.

Writers' conferences can be helpful. Something you hear at one may come to mind months or years later when you are struggling with a writing problem. But writers' conferences, like other human institutions, vary in value. While their directors try to get the best talent they can, they sometimes enlist successful writers who are very poor teachers and lecturers. Some conferences are heavily weighted with persons of mature years but no serious literary prospects. Other conferences give the conferees too much starry-eyed inspiration and not enough realistic information.

Preparation for writing by means of books, courses, and conferences will save the writer from making ghastly mistakes. One well-educated would-be author, for instance, spent years on a utopian novel, which, when we saw the manuscript, was utterly hopeless. The author had no notion of how to tell a story, and the result was stupefyingly dull. The writer's errors were so obvious that any professional could have pointed them out to him in a matter of minutes. He would have been better off if he had never started this foredoomed venture at all.

There is some danger that, by forming a taste for books, courses, and conferences on writing, you may spend your whole life on them and never get around to writing. Then you would be like the "perpetual student" of whom nineteenth-century European writers and dramatists used to make fun.

☆ ☆ ☆

What basic skills and equipment do you need for profes-

PREPARING FOR A SCIENCE-FICTION CAREER

sional writing, besides knowledge of English and the techniques of fiction?

You should know touch typing. There may still be writers who write in longhand, but they mostly belong to an older generation and must have their manuscripts typed professionally before submission. There are also some who type by hunting and pecking. Although some have become fairly skilled at two-finger typing, it is still slower than touch typing. A modern writer who cannot type with all his fingers is like a cowboy who cannot ride a horse.

Shorthand, which you can teach yourself, is very useful. Even if you never become adept enough at it to be a court stenographer, it is helpful for taking notes and outlining.

You will, of course, need a good typewriter. Different kinds (manual or electric, standard or portable) have various advantages and disadvantages. Sprague de Camp has some of the symbols removed and the diacritical marks ´ , ` , ¨ , ^ , and ~ installed, since he has many occasions to use foreign words and names, and it is much easier to type in these symbols than to insert them after typing. Square brackets are also useful.

Use an all-black ribbon; the red half of a red-and-black ribbon is virtually useless. Change your ribbon often; editors are annoyed by manuscripts typed with pallid, inkless ribbons.

You will want a big dictionary. Small ones are not of much use, because you already know most of the words in them. If you can afford it, get a good encyclopedia. A second-hand set, in good condition, of the fourteenth edition of the *Encyclopaedia Britannica* might be an excellent buy.

You will also need a thesaurus, a book of familiar quotations (such as *Bartlett's*), a good atlas, and perhaps a recent issue of one of the world almanacs published by several leading newspapers. A recent edition of the Chemical Rubber Company's *Handbook of Chemistry and Physics* may solve many little scientific problems arising in writing science fiction. A recent issue of *Writer's Market* (published by *Writer's Digest* of Cincinnati) is helpful in investigating markets. Handy for a writer or connoisseur of imaginative fiction are several indexes of the stories appearing in science-fiction and fantasy magazines over the last half-century.

You also need one or more filing cabinets and a well-developed filing system, of which we shall have more to say later. And of course you need a place to write in, be it in your apartment, or a space that you rent.

☆ ☆ ☆

What special knowledge do you need to write imaginative fiction, as opposed to fiction in general? You need not be a scientist yourself, but you should certainly know more than your readers about the subjects that you discuss, and your readers include some pretty intelligent people.

A scientific or technical education is very useful to a science-fiction writer. A non-technical man can, however, pick up enough science to write a science-fiction story, albeit it may take some digging. Seldom need you go far into the more abstruse and mathematical aspects of the science. A writer can find plenty of popularizations of almost any science, and there are many good scientific periodicals: *Archaeology, Engineering and Science, Expedition, Natural History, Science, Science Digest, Scientific American,* and *Smithsonian,* to mention some leaders in the field. Nobody can keep up with all of these, but you should follow at least a few of them regularly.

If you have no technical background and have not acquired a solid amateur's grounding in science, you had better stay away from highly technical, gadgety stories and rely for your appeal more on human interest, exciting action, or the glamor of exotic settings.

Can you know too much about a subject, to the point where your knowledge hampers your imagination or weighs down the action? No. You will not live long enough to learn all the things that might be useful in your writing. Knowing scientific facts, however, does not mean dragging all of them into your stories merely to show off your erudition. One should never put anything into a story for that reason.

So a writer must never be afraid to get in and dig. One of the greatest curses of writers is sheer dumb ignorance. Often, they simply do not know enough about their fellow men and the universe in which they live to avoid glaring mistakes of fact and lapses of logic. One writer has put dinosaurs, which were air-breathers like us, at the bottom of the ocean. Another has caused his hero to swing a fifty-pound sword, a feat beyond the thews even of Conan the Cimmerian. A third has referred to an oriental character named ibn-Hasan as "Ibn," which is like calling a man named Johnson "Son." And writers still tell of corpses whose faces bear expressions of "indescribable horror," as though the faces of corpses had any expression at all.

Do you think that nobody but a pedant cares for such petty details, least of all the average reader? Then you are wrong. Even if the reader does not know about the weight of swords and the grammar of Arabic, such a lapse is likely to give him an uneasy feeling that something, he knows not what, is wrong. And pop! goes the illusion that the writer has sought to build up.

Details are especially important in an imaginative story, because the reader's suspension of disbelief is already under strain. He has been hauled from his own familiar little world to Alpha Centauri, Atlantis, the millionth century, or a parallel universe. Therefore the least fallacy or inconsistency is likely to cause the illusion to snap like an overstretched rubber band.

Some writers have been successful without much factual knowledge; Edgar Rice Burroughs, for example. They have, however, achieved this success by virtues that more than make up for their faults. You are advised to imitate their virtues, not their faults. You will have enough faults of your own without borrowing others'.

A writer can, by careful research, compose a surprisingly plausible picture of an environment in which he has never been. Although it is easier to write convincingly of a place the writer has seen than of one he has not, and of an experience he has undergone than of one he has not, nobody lives long enough to get all the experiences that would be useful in writing.

For example, one of Sprague de Camp's early stories, "The

Blue Giraffe," was laid in South Africa, where at that time he had never been. By a bit of library research and conversation with an Afrikander friend, he worked up so much authentic local color that a reader wrote from South Africa, saying it was plain that the writer had once lived "in this sunny land of ours."

On the other hand, it is hard to avoid all mistakes. Sprague de Camp's novel *Lest Darkness Fall* put his modern hero back into sixth-century Rome. To lend authenticity, he had a couple of his characters utter a few phrases in the Gothic language. After the book appeared, he got a letter from a professor, praising the story but adding that he had caused his Goths to use the nominative case when they should have used the vocative!

☆ ☆ ☆

Having acquired the knowledge and equipment for writing imaginative fiction, what do you do next?

It is an axiom of professional writing that no editor ever bought a story that was not written, or which, if written, was never submitted. So you must write.

However, unless you are independently rich, or have a wife who can support you while you are getting started, you had better keep your job and write in your spare time until you are well established. This is likely to be hard on family life.

Moreover, you should not expect to sell to the highest-paying markets at the start. It has been done, but the chances are against it. A friend of ours, a scientist of literary talents, once undertook to become a writer by flouting both these rules. Although he had never sold a story, he quit his job and sat down at his typewriter to write fantasies. Being a slow worker, he thought he would have to sell to the slick-paper magazines to make a living. Advice to the contrary he politely but firmly brushed off.

The only trouble with this scheme was that the slick-paper magazines would not coöperate. After a year of writing without a single sale, our friend had spent all the money that he had saved for this enterprise and had to go back to the laboratories.

So now Saturday morning has come and the spare room

has been converted to a studio by installing your typewriter, stationery supplies, and reference books. What do you write?

SCIENCE FICTION HANDBOOK, REVISED

THOSE CRAZY IDEAS

People who write imaginative fiction are often asked: Where do you get those crazy ideas? Let us consider where writers do get them.

To any professional, the obvious answer is that, if we knew, we should go back there for more. Strictly speaking, we do not get them. They come to us. They come while we are walking, bathing, going to sleep, or doing anything else that does not call for close concentration.

Professional writers have no monopoly on fictionally usable thoughts. Most intelligent people have interesting ideas. But, whereas most people forget them, the professional carries a pad or notebook in which he makes notes of stray ideas. When he gets back to his study, he types them out and files them. Then, when he sets himself to write a story, without a clear knowledge of what the story will be, he glances through the file to see if he has something there that will serve his purpose.

For example: a couple of decades ago, our older son, then aged nine, announced that his school was putting on the opera *Hansel and Gretel,* and wouldn't we come? (Since a writer is self-employed and makes his own schedule, everybody thinks that he is available at any time.) We allowed our arms to be twisted and in due course found ourselves in a large, bare room with a stage at one end, sitting in a row with all the other mothers.

Sprague de Camp does not greatly enjoy watching a bunch

of fourth-graders hopping about to the tune of Humperdinck's mediocre music. He was suffering silently when Catherine whispered:

"Cheer up; it's only half an hour more."

With a sigh, he replied: "Yes, people go thousands of miles to see primitives performing tribal rites, and here such a rite is under way just a few blocks from home."

"In fact," continued Catherine, "I'll bet you make a story of it."

"By God, I will!" Sprague said. Then he thought: "How would it be if a chair in the rear row were occupied by an extraterrestrial visitor, who had come from some far world to witness *our* tribal rites?"

He made a note of the idea and, when he got home, typed it out. A year later, the idea became the story "Proposal."

☆ ☆ ☆

This account makes the process seem simpler than it is. When you first sit down to write, you may not have any ideas in the file. Moreover, a bare idea, such as that of an extraterrestrial at a school play, is not a story. So let us look more closely at what a story is.

A story is a new combination of old elements, which have entered the writer's mind through his senses. No author ever wrote anything completely new. What he wrote was, at best, a new combination of old elements. Sprague de Camp had seen the performance of *Hansel and Gretel*; he had read plenty of stories about extraterrestrials; and he also threw in a well-founded item of local gossip. After stewing and stirring, the story took form.

Two factors enter into the building of a viable story idea: the experiences that the writer has had, which serve as the raw material for his combinations; and his creative imagination, which picks these experiences out of his memory and combines them into a plot.

Before your creative imagination can work, it needs experience to work on. All fiction could be broken down into bits of the writer's experience, if we knew enough about the writer's life. Samuel Taylor Coleridge's *Kubla Khan* and *The Ancient Mariner* have been traced by John Livingstone

Lowes, in *The Road to Xanadu,* to old travel books that Coleridge had read. Thus "Alph, the sacred river," comes from the Alpheios River in western Greece, about which legends were told in Classical times. "His flashing eyes, his floating hair" is from an account of the king of Ethiopia by James Bruce, the eighteenth-century Scottish explorer.

Experience can be either personal or vicarious. Vicarious experience is what you have heard of, read of, or seen in dramatic form. For story material, personal experience is much the best. There is no preparation for writing about a typhoon, a battle, a surgical operation, or a love affair that compares to having been through one.

Unless, however, one is extraordinarily active, energetic, and versatile over a number of years, it takes a lifetime to gather enough personal experience for a full-time writing career. This is why we find a pearl fisherman, or a railroad conductor, or a steel puddler who writes just one novel based upon his environment or occupation. His story may be publishable or even excellent. But, having written it, the man has shot his bolt. Sometimes, misled by initial success, such a one-shot author sets himself up as a full-time professional only to find that he is writing the same story over and over.

If the would-be writer, on the other hand, spends too many decades acquiring first-hand experience in a number of fields, he will not have the time to learn to write. Hence many explorers, adventurers, and intelligence agents have fascinating stories to tell but cannot tell them in publishable form without the help of a ghost writer.

Still, every bit of personal experience, no matter how painful at the time, can sooner or later be turned to account in your writing. Thus Theodore Sturgeon used his employment on earth-moving machinery in his "Killdozer." A. Bertram Chandler, a merchant-marine captain, has long exploited his nautical experience in his fiction. Having worked in a sawmill, a correspondence school, a trade-journal publishing company, and an engineering laboratory, Sprague de Camp has insinuated all four backgrounds into his own tales.

Because first-hand experience is so valuable, it is usually

better for a young, aspiring writer not to plunge into full-time writing as soon as he finishes his formal education. Since his creative imagination will have a comparatively meager stock of experiences to draw upon, the combinations that it builds into stories will seem feeble and trite.

Yet, a writer should not wait too long before starting to write. Creative imagination varies with time. With many, it seems to reach its peak in late adolescence or early adulthood and thereafter slowly to decline. Hence many writers start out with a stock of highly original ideas but express them in crude, verbose style. As they get older, they learn to express themselves more clearly and elegantly, but their ideas become less original. With each new story, they have to struggle harder not to repeat themselves. As an editor once shrewdly observed, fiction writing is the only craft that gets harder with practice.[1]

Now you see why it is wise for a fledgling writer to start writing as a spare-time occupation while working at a regular job. The writing gives him practice and enables him to set down his most original ideas, while the job furnishes him with experience of the real world and enables him to go on eating. When he reaches his thirties or forties, has had a variety of experience, has money in the bank, and knows that he can sell practically everything he writes, he can start thinking of full-time free-lancing.

Sometimes, even a mature writer has an unpleasant surprise. He has figured that, if he turns out so many pages by spending five hours a week at part-time writing, he will produce ten times as much salable copy by working fifty hours a week. Writing, however, does not work that way. The writer soon runs into a law of diminishing returns and may find himself able to turn out only twice or thrice as much salable material as he could while moonlighting.

There remains vicarious experience, which is even more important in imaginative than in realistic fiction. Since nobody can yet ship as a hand on a space ship to the planets of another star or travel into the future or to a parallel universe, experience of these things must perforce be vicarious.

Practically speaking, this means wide and systematic reading. Since most writers are heavy readers to begin with, no urging should be needed. If you have read this far, you are probably enthusiastic enough about imaginative fiction to read much of it regularly.

To get the needed knowledge of your fellow men and of the real universe, you should also put in solid stints of non-fiction reading. There are plenty of books of popularized science from which a non-technical writer can profit. You need not master the entire field of the sciences—nobody could do that—but you should have a smattering of all the major branches and a good amateur's working knowledge of some.

Some years ago, Dr. Eric Temple Bell divided technical knowledge into the physical sciences, the biological (including the social and historical) sciences, and engineering. He advised writers to specialize in one of these three. He also warned writers against "fossil" or outdated science and urged them to look at the date of everything they read.[2] The rate of obsolescence of a science depends on how fast it progresses. Our knowledge of history, for instance, changes but slowly, while a five-year-old book on atomic physics already shows signs of senility.

Lastly, it is good to devote at least some time to reading contemporary fiction outside the imaginative field. Thus one learns modern fictional techniques and comes upon ideas usable in quite different contexts. While it would be presumptuous for us to tell anyone else what to read, an ideal reading schedule might comprise one third imaginative fiction, one third realistic fiction, and one third non-fiction— mainly science, history, and biography.

Bernard De Voto once remarked that reading is one of the few pure amateur forms of enjoyment, without ulterior motives—except for professional writers. When you become a professional, you give up this pleasure, at least in its purest form, because everything you read must be scrutinized for what use you can make of it.[3] If you are systematic, you will take notes on every important book that you read and keep scrapbooks of newspaper clippings and magazine tear sheets about all the subjects that interest you. We have a file of several thousand 3" x 5" index cards, listing articles in magazines, which we have kept and filed away in an orderly manner in storage boxes. Such files become extremely helpful when they have accumulated for a few years.

☆ ☆ ☆

Having gained experience, the writer must take the next step. He must induce his imagination to assemble his fancies into usable form. Creative imagination is the catalyst, the mysterious agent, of the fiction-writing process. It is spoken of in reverent tones at writers' conferences and in articles on How To Write. People who claim to have it sometimes use it as an affectation or as an excuse for behavior that might otherwise be deemed merely eccentric. But just what it is is less certain.

Is creative imagination restricted to writers? No; artists of all sorts, inventors, scientists, craftsmen, promoters, advertisers, and even some political and military leaders have it—anybody, that is, who gives the world something new and different.

Can one write fiction without it? Sometimes, but the result is likely to be reviewed with such cold-potato phrases as "competent journalism."

Is creative imagination a reliable or predictable human attribute, like brown eyes? No. It crops up in the unlikeliest social settings. It disappears or goes on strike in the midst of a writer's career, perhaps to return, perhaps not. And when it becomes exhausted, as it usually does if the writer lives long enough, the writer finds himself willy-nilly writing the same story again and again.

If creative imagination is important to the writer of realistic fiction, it is *a fortiori* important to the author of imaginative fiction. For whatever such a writer can do, he can hardly just report things as they are and claim to have an imaginative story. Of course, an unimaginative writer can plagiarize the works of his colleagues, but such conduct is no more approved in this field than in any other branch of fiction.

Bernard De Voto, in *The World of Fiction,* asserted that

the absolute essential for successful fiction-writing was neither profound erudition, nor painstaking research, nor warm human sympathy, nor technical writing skill, useful though all these qualities be. It was, rather, the ability to visualize one's characters, setting, and events so vividly and intensely that the reader is forced to share in this act of imagination. His attention is so completely seized that it is dragged along with the story willy-nilly. This is the quality that we are discussing. The fact that some have it, while others do not, explains why some writers, whose writings contain egregious faults, nevertheless capture a large and lasting readership; while others, whose writing is technically polished and whose ideas sound promising, never make it.

Creative imagination seems to be a development of the faculty of free association. You may have once undergone a free-association test at the desk of a psychologist, who shot words at you while you answered with the first words that popped into your head. This test classifies you roughly as an extravert or an introvert and uncovers subjects about which you have strong emotions such as guilt or fear.

He who has creative imagination can, for every concept, quickly conjure up a large number and variety of associated terms, experimentally join them in a multitude of combinations, and choose those combinations most pregnant with fictional possibilities. It makes little difference to the final result whether this process takes place on the conscious or the unconscious level. Robert Moore Williams once wrote us, explaining how it works:

> This imagination is a remarkable gizmo. Once you learn how to watch it at work, to see it or listen to it—whichever way it works for you—it will synthesize and present for your inspection an unlimited number of stories in an endless variety. The trick is to learn how to recognize it, to unblock for it, to get out of its way. This imagination is a most astounding thing. . . . It will handle tremendous numbers of facts and correlate them in a manner that makes these electric computers look like tinker toys. Also it seems to

work with the speed of light. ... To make this gizmo a little clearer, 1 will say that it is working on a one-volt charge. ... But the rest of the human organism seems to have a hundred-volt charge. In the face of this hundred-volt pressure, the little old one-volt charge of Mr. Imagination gets pretty badly lost unless you have learned how to sidetrack the hundred-volt charge and get it out of the way so the one-volt charge can get through and is available to you. This is the still, small voice that you want to hear and the trick of all writing and all other creative effort is the trick of learning how to listen to this still, small voice that operates on a one-volt charge. How do you do it? Just listen.

After you have sweated for days, consciously trying out hopeless-seeming combinations of ideas, the right combination may suddenly pop into your unconscious mind, causing you to wonder how you could have been so stupid as not to have seen it sooner.

Since your imagination is mostly down in your unconscious where you cannot get at it, you cannot force it to do anything. You can only set the stage for it and hope that it feels like working. It can sometimes be stimulated with caffein, although we should not advise you to rely on stimulants of any sort.

Alcohol is very dangerous to the imagination. One who gets into the habit of drinking before writing becomes unable to compose without alcohol and finally unable to compose even with it. We are not, ourselves, abstainers from social drinking, but we have seen the effect of the injudicious use of liquor on too many of our colleagues to have illusions about mixing alcohol and writing.

The same applies, even more strongly, to the use of cannabin, the active agent in marijuana and hashish. There is much inconclusive argument about the effects of marijuana. From all we have read and heard and observed, we are inclined to think that it does the following: First, it lowers the user's general level of energy and ambition; in ordinary language, it tends to make him lazy. If there is any quality that a writer does not need, laziness is it. Second, it tends to destroy his faculty of self-criticism, so that he cannot tell whether he is writing good copy or bilge. Since the latter is easier, he soon comes to write bilge all the time. Third, these effects appear to be long-lasting if not altogether permanent. We are not being dogmatic about this controversial subject, but this is the direction in which the evidence so far presented tends to incline us.

With most writers, the creative process requires much undisturbed time—many hours at a stretch without distractions. One of a writer's less agreeable tasks is to train his nearest and dearest not to burst in on him with questions like: "Where is the checkbook, dear?" or "Daddy, how about driving me to the movies?" We have known authors who could write in odd moments or work in the midst of a roaring party, but they are not typical.

Once, years ago, our late friend Willy Ley, who was quite successful as a non-fiction writer and who had sold some science fiction, got financially pinched. We urged him to try some more fiction. He had tried, he said, but it did no good. No ideas.

How long did he try? we asked. Oh, a couple of hours at a time. We had to explain that it usually took at least a week or two to conceive and plot a short story and a month or two or even more to outline a novel.

The imagination's leisurely and capricious working habits are a constant source of irritation to spouses of fiction writers, unless they, too, become authors. Every so often, the fiction writer seems to go into a trance. He sits all day with pencil in hand, clip board on lap, and vacant expression on face. Although he seems to be doing absolutely nothing, he insists that he is working hard and must on no account be interrupted.

What goes on during this trance? That depends upon the writer. Some start with ideas of one kind, some with another.

The creator of Captain Hornblower pointed out that the adventure-story writer conceives an event or a train of events and then devises characters to fit them, whereas the non-adventure-story writer is apt to think up his characters first and let these characters do what persons of their kind would naturally do. As most stories of imaginative fiction belong in the adventure category, we suppose that most writers of science fiction and fantasy use the former approach. The result is that most imaginative stories do not fall into that class of character-centered stories which many literary critics regard as the worthiest type of fiction.

We should say that, important though character be in stories and significant though character-centered stories be, the question of character is sometimes overstressed. A good character-centered story can be very absorbing, but so can a good idea-centered, action-centered, or setting-centered story. Moreover, when a story of character is badly written, it can be at least as tedious as a bad story of one of the other kinds.

We have heard it said that historical romances (at present somewhat out of style) are largely written by people who, lacking the most acute sense of, or feeling for, character, put their stories in exotic settings, where the costumery and pageantry make up for this lack. There may be something to this. But it does not necessarily follow that the character-centered story is inherently better than all the others; any more than, as H. P. Lovecraft was always asserting, the story centered on mood and atmosphere is the only one with any true "art." Most imaginative stories are in fact idea-centered, action-centered, or setting-centered.

Sprague de Camp has used all these approaches. He has often conceived a story first in the form of a problem: What *if* something happened to make all mankind grow long hair all over, like monkeys? Or he might start with a single imagined event, such as the extraterrestrial at the school play. Or he might conceive a story first in terms of its setting, as with his stories of the *Viagens Interplanetarias*.

While he thinks of many characters—usually combining attributes of different people whom he has known—rarely do the characters themselves form the basis for a story. They are more likely to sit in the idea file until a story comes along in which they can play an appropriate part. Other writers use different systems.

During his trance, a writer does not merely indulge in idle reverie. For fictional use, the imagination must be disciplined to serve certain ends. The writer is trying to do three things: to entertain the reader, to express himself and his feelings, and to convey some idea or opinion. These objectives vary according to the writer's personality and experience. Still, the proportions in which these ingredients are mixed determines the kind of story that results.

For instance, in Burroughs the entertainment element predominates. In Bradbury and Ellison, we get a strong flavor of the author's personality; we might call these "self-expression stories." In Heinlein and Asimov, the element of serious, logical thought is strong. While all these elements are found in all stories, most authors tend to stress one over the others. To overstress any one may, however, cause trouble. The story of pure entertainment becomes a "contrived" or "formula" story; the story of pure self-expression becomes unintelligible; the story of pure cerebration comes across as a thinly disguised non-fiction article.

☆ ☆ ☆

Writers are sometimes asked if it is practical for one person—usually somebody with no writing experience—to furnish ideas and the other to do the writing. We strongly advise any writer who can write his own tales not to entertain such a proposal. For one thing, so many imaginative stories have now been published that really new ideas are rare. Nearly everything written uses ideas that have seen print before. The novelty consists merely of the writer's originality of plotting, treatment, and expression.

It follows that most of the ideas that a self-styled idea man would submit would be old, and the writer could find them by digging through files of old magazines. Since they would, however, be new to the idea man, he would believe them new in fact and would claim a share of the profits if the writer ever used them thereafter. Suppose for instance, that the idea man suggested the following:

An expedition lands on a strange planet, where the flat, swampy landscape is covered with scattered ponds and huge night-blooming flowers.

The men build a large hut, which they use as a base. Just as they finish it, they begin to disappear at night. Watches are posted, but the sentries always fall asleep. When a man is missing in the morning, the explorers scour the landscape but find no trace of him. At last, the expedition leader discovers that the night-blooming flowers give forth a soporific perfume. By clearing away the flowers from around the hut and using a medical stimulant, he stays awake when all the rest go to sleep. A huge arm comes through the window and gropes around, until the leader burns it off with his heat-ray gun and hears the monster shamble off in the darkness. Next day, he tracks it to the edge of a pond. With diving apparatus, he plunges to the bottom of the pond, where he finds the mutilated monster's corpse, and its mate, alive, awaiting him. . . .

Now surely you recognize the source of that story? (If you do not, you have not done enough homework.) It is simply the Anglo-Saxon epic *Beowulf*, retold in an interplanetary setting. Nobody, certainly, has a copyright on *Beowulf*, and a writer is foolish to put himself in a position where anybody might claim to have sold him an idea that has been public property for a thousand years.

Then how is collaboration accomplished? People have asked: "Mr. de Camp, how did you collaborate with Fletcher Pratt? Which one did what?"

He tells them: "First, Pratt and I got together to plot and outline a story. After an hour or two of tossing ideas back and forth, I would depart with a sheet of shorthand notes to write a rough draft at home. I sent this to Pratt, who wrote the final draft, sent me a copy for criticism and correction, and submitted another to the publisher. Sometimes we varied the procedure. If he knew much more about the subject than I, he might do the rough draft and I, the final. Either of us might make changes in the other's finished work."

With other collaborators, the proceedings may be further varied. Thus, when Willy Ley and Sprague de Camp wrote their non-fiction *Lands Beyond,* each wrote half the chapters and rewrote what the other had done.

The de Camps, who have collaborated on eight books to date, follow both procedures. In the present book, for example, Catherine has rewritten Sprague's original text and, being the business manager for the writing team, has added a chapter on the business side of the writing profession.

Collaboration works best when the collaborators make contributions of equal importance and when their special skills complement, rather than duplicate, each other. When one collaborator is considerably older than the other, it is usually best for the younger to do the rough draft. The younger writer is likely to be more fertile and facile, while the older is probably the keener critic, with a sharper eye for inconsistencies, grammatical errors, and other flaws. If they make contributions of more or less equal importance, it is usual to divide the profits half and half.

There is no point in collaboration merely for its own sake. If the joint product of two minds is no better than that of one, each collaborator will find that he has halved his reward for almost the same amount of effort. Moreover, neither enjoys the satisfaction of single-handed creativity. And we might as well face the fact that one of the rewards of authorship, which makes up for its other disadvantages like financial insecurity, is the satisfaction of normal human vanity—the thrill of being able to say: I, and nobody else, did this!

PLOTTING

AN IMAGINATIVE STORY

Anyone who tries to teach others how to write should remember Kipling's ballad, "In the Neolithic Age," wherein the poet tells how, in a primitive incarnation, he liquidated critics of his verse:

> Then I stripped them, scalp from skull, and my
>   hunting dogs fed full,
> And their teeth I threaded neatly on a thong:
> And I wiped my mouth and said, "It is well that
>   they are dead,
> For I know my work is right and theirs was
>   wrong."

> But my totem saw the shame; from his ridgepole
>   shrine he came,
> And he told me in a vision of the night:—
> "There are nine and sixty ways of constructing
>   tribal lays,
> And every single one of them is right!"

We can show how some have written stories successfully and suggest that their methods are sound. Of course, the job could be done in other ways. Writers have broken all the rules and still sold their stories. If, when you have finished reading this chapter, you wish to break the rules, go ahead and follow your own bent. Perhaps your method will work too. Still, in story writing as elsewhere, you stand a better chance of success if you know the rules before you start to break them.

Writers vary in the way they build a plot. One outlines his story on paper; another, having already composed the story in his head, just sits down and writes. One knows in advance exactly what will happen in the story before he begins writing; another has only a rough idea and solves his plot problems as they arise.

The writer who believes that he does not plot his story at all in advance is mistaken. He is plotting it, but on a subconscious level. As long as his unconscious can keep ahead of his typewriter, well and good. Sprague de Camp belongs to the careful-planning school. He has found this method most successful and thinks it on the whole best suited to imaginative fiction, at least to action-centered and idea-centered stories, which between them make up a large majority of all imaginative tales. On a very few occasions, a story has come to him in such complete form that it practically wrote itself, without advance outlining, but this is rare.

Usually, when Sprague plots, he outlines the story in pencil until it is thoroughly formed. This gestation period may take anywhere from a day to a week for a short story and from one to two months for a novel. When he has his story lined up and his characters and incidents all accounted for, he types a complete outline, which may run from half a page for a short story to several pages for a novel. A sample plot plan appears on the following page.

Next, Sprague types a rough draft, makes drastic corrections, retypes, and further revises the work. Then comes the final draft. For a book-length work, he usually has the final draft typed by a professional typist For shorter works, the second draft can often be converted into a final draft by retyping such sections as require substantial changes, substituting them for the incorrect passages by cutting and pasting, and making a photocopy of the whole.

Writers sometimes affect being more spontaneous and disorganized than they really are. This is no doubt a hangover of nineteenth-century romanticism, when a writer was deemed a person of too beautiful a soul, too delicate a sensitivity, and too preoccupied a mind to bother with such mundane matters as getting his hair cut or paying his bills.

PLOTTING AN IMAGINATIVE STORY
SAMPLE PLOT PLAN

BALSAMO'S MIRROR -- short story --

Chief character: H. P. Lovecraft, unnamed.
Story told by Wilson Newbury as an MIT student,
c. 1934.

HPL talks about the XVIIIth cent.; disillusioned when he sees it in fact.

HPL & WN go on nocturnal walk in Providence. Visit medium, Mme. Nosi. She sends them back
to +XVIII bodies by means of magic mirror.

Find selves in bodies of Somersetshire farmer & son, but cannot communicate. Read Field-
ing, Sheridan, Sterne for dialects.

Time: c. 1765. Bodies named "Philip" and
"William" respectively.

Phil & Will on way to fair. Phil has feud
with local squire, who wants to buy his land.
Phil a self-educated Wesleyan.

Phil warned by friendly landowner at fair.
Meets squire, Sir Roger, & son. Squire bids
Phil to mansion for business talk.

Confrontation at mansion. Phil & Will defy
Roger & walk out. Phil & Will set out to poach
on Roger's land. Caught in act by Roger & son &
killed.

HPL & Will back in own bodies. Mirror broken. Mme. Nosi dead (heart?). Police; investi-
gation. HPL disillusioned with all human eras.
Will journey only to dreamland thereafter.

The main objection to the technique of just sitting down and writing is that, while it sometimes produces effective stories, it often strands the writer halfway through with the horrid realization that his tale has fallen apart, that he has no idea of what is coming next, or that he has written himself into a corner whence there is no escape.

☆ ☆ ☆

A story normally has a structure, even though this fact may be artfully concealed. If a story lacks structure, it will seem formless, forceless, and pointless, as indeed do many of the stories of the "New Wave." Few editors have much use for a story that merely states a situation without doing anything about it.

The plot of a story is its skeleton—an outline or synopsis of the theme and incidents in the story. Teachers of writing sometimes distinguish between the plot of a story and the story line. The former is a résumé of all the major ideas and events that are stated or implied in the story; the latter, of only those incidents that take place onstage. A story always implies much more than it states. Most characters, for instance, have pasts that stretch back to their birth, of which fragments still adhere to them. So only a fraction of "what happens" is narrated in detail. The reader fills in the rest.

There are those who do not believe that a story should have plot. This attitude is found among some of the academics who have lately been drafted into teaching imaginative fiction without knowing much about it. Lester del Rey tells how he

> ... went to lecture at a workshop conducted by a local college. The teacher did know something of science fiction but didn't seem to care much for it. He grew increasingly unhappy as I answered a question from one student about the structure of a story that would sell to a magazine. When I finally used the nasty word *plot*, he could stand it no longer. "Oh," he broke in, "you're talking about what we call good story!" He sniffed in contempt. "We don't teach that here."[1]

If you prefer to write merely as a form of self-expression,

without thought of the reader, that is your privilege. There is no law against it. If the resulting story slumbers peacefully in your files until your heirs throw it out with the trash, that is all right, too. We are writing, however, for would-be authors who mean to practice the trade in a professional manner—to write stories to entertain the reader, to get them published, and to get paid for them.

A story is a narrative about people feeling and doing things—or, if it is an imaginative story, about sentient beings feeling and doing things. Your hero may just as well be a robot, a flying saucerian, an intellectual animal, or a ghoul.

Since yours is an imaginative story, it is based upon some assumption contrary to present-day knowledge or belief. H. G. Wells pointed out that he owed part of his success to the fact that he restricted himself to one assumption per story:

> The thing that makes such imaginations interesting is their translation into commonplace terms and a rigid exclusion of other marvels from the story. Then it becomes human. "How would you feel and what might not happen to you," is the typical question, if for instance pigs could fly and one came rocketing over a hedge at you. How would you feel and what might not happen to you if suddenly you were changed into an ass and couldn't tell anyone about it? Or if you suddenly became invisible? But no one would think twice about the answer if hedges and houses also began to fly, or if people changed into lions, tigers, cats and dogs left and right, or if anyone could vanish anyhow. Nothing remains interesting where anything may happen.[2]

This one assumption may be as narrow as assuming that a professor develops equations that tell whether a club or society will grow or shrink, once he knows its organization,[3] or as broad as a galactic empire. But it is still one assumption. If you try to work in two or more independent assumptions, your story is likely to crumble between them.

Therefore, limit your assumptions to one major concept,

which may include any number of minor ones growing out of and consistent with it. Do not devote the first half of your story to a realistic description of a flight to some distant planet and then turn your tale into a ghost story with an extraterrestrial locale.

Fletcher Pratt once asserted that the science-fiction writer should not violate any established scientific fact, "except where the violation itself constitutes the basis of the story and a plausible explanation is furnished. . . . No special phenomena just for effect." Likewise the fantasy writer should obey the rule that "no established fact of normal psychological behavior may be violated except under the same conditions as above."[4] These are good working principles, although many authors violate them. Thus, time travel is often taken for granted, as if it were a truly possible form of transportation, which elementary logic tells us it is not.

☆ ☆ ☆

During the construction of a story, you must choose a title. Give the story a title that has something to do with the story but that does not add to the story or form a necessary part of it. Such titles confess a weakness in the story. If the story has a surprise ending, do not use a title that gives the point away.

Titles should not be too long. Six or seven words are plenty; one word is good if you can find the right word. Titles should not be unpronounceable, like David R. Sparks's "Ape Men of Xlotli." If you can put some paradox or incongruity into the title, as in Hubbard's "The Case of the Friendly Corpse," so much the better. Alliterative or rhyming titles, like Patrick Dutton's "The Beautiful Bacillus," are good.

It might be wise to check the indexes to stories in science-fiction and fantasy magazines, to make sure that you have not chosen a title already used. While not fatal or even illegal, such a gaffe can prove embarrassing.

Every good story has a beginning, a middle, a turning point, and an end. Writers define these elements as an opening, a development, a climax, and a denouement. If the story lacks any of these elements, the reader may have trouble making sense of it.

The *opening* of a story, which may constitute anywhere from one to fifty pages, gets the reader oriented. It tells him where and when the action takes place and what is happening to whom. It sets the general tone of the story and enables the reader to identify himself with the leading character. It usually includes a "narrative hook"—a statement or phrase intended to catch the reader's interest.

Many writers have trouble in deciding where to start their stories. They either start them too early, so that the reader has to plow through a lot of dull introductory material, which could be thrown out or reduced to a few sentences; or they start them too late, in which case they have to recapitulate essential antecedent facts in long flashbacks. More often, they start too early and waste many pages fiddling around with irrelevant action and unnecessary description before they get into the story proper. The rule, if there can be said to be a rule, is that you start your story as late as you can without having an awkward lot of antecedent material to work in.

Then comes the *development*. This usually makes up the bulk of the story—perhaps more than nine tenths. At the start of the tale, it has been established that somebody (or some Thing) is pursuing an objective, even though this objective may be merely to escape from a threat or predicament. During the development, obstacles arise to frustrate or endanger the protagonist. Perhaps the author has two opposed protagonists, each constituting the other's obstacle.

To hold the reader's interest, you should make the objective something that really matters to the protagonist, something that he wants badly. If he does not care, neither will the reader. Moreover, do not make the attainment of his goal too easy. Wilmar Shiras wrote a strong novelette for *Astounding,* "In Hiding," about the troubles of a mutant superboy. Then in the sequel, "Opening Doors," everything comes so easily to her supergirl heroine that the story falls flat. If the hero is a flawless and invincible superman, the reader will think: "Of course, good old Lazarus Conan

Kinnison will beat the Things and save the galaxy," and he will stifle a yawn.

During the development, the writer brings in all those complications and incidents that are thought of as "plot." In assembling these incidents, try to omit any that have no real connection with the main theme of the story, even though writers of extraverted pure-adventure stories often indulge in action for its own sake.

Furthermore, avoid using one standardized incident in many different stories. It is easy to make this mistake without realizing it. Burroughs's Martian heroes and heroines are always setting out in a "flier" at the beginning and getting shot down or wrecked in a wild part of Mars. In 1941, Sprague de Camp wrote a light fantasy novel, *The Undesired Princess,* in which the hero, in a strange "dimension," is taken on a burlesque hunting party and falls off his mount. Years later, he wrote a science-fiction novel, *The Queen of Zamba,*[5] whose hero, on a strange planet, is taken on a burlesque hunting party and falls off his mount. When he wrote the second story, he had forgotten all about this incident in the first and was reminded of it only when he read galley proofs for the book version of *The Undesired Princess.*

During the development, the action builds up to a *climax.* Then the question is decided: does the protagonist get what he is after or not? Does he escape his doom or not?

In a short story, you have room for only one climax. In a novel, on the other hand, you may have several. In such a case, it is wise to reserve the most important one to the last. The story should be so managed that the reader cannot foresee the outcome of the climax; but at the same time, when he does reach the end, he realizes that the story turned out as it inevitably had to and that all the premises from which the conclusion followed were openly shown to him early in the tale.

After the climax, there are usually a few more things to be said: mysteries to be explained, loose ends to be tidied up, morals or philosophical inferences to be drawn by the surviving characters, and perhaps a hint of what happened after that. This coda is the *denouement,* which occurs in its most formal form in the standard detective story. The disclosure of the murderer is the climax, and the detective's explanation is the denouement.

Imaginative stories do not follow this pattern so rigidly, but these elements will still be found in nearly all published stories. Sometimes the denouement, instead of following the climax, will be worked in ahead of it. All the questions have already been answered, so that when the universe blows up there is no need for further explanations. Or the story may deliberately end on a questioning note: the Aliens, as they depart, say: "You have won this time, Earth Creatures, but we shall return!"

Ending a story on a questioning note is one thing; leaving everything so vague that the reader never finds out what happened is another. A common and easy method of arousing reader interest or working up an atmosphere of suspense is to have strange, apparently inexplicable things happen in a normal setting, or to throw dark hints that behind the façade of the normal there lurk horrors too frightful for description. But what do you do then? Chambers, Machen, and Lovecraft were all given to this approach and encountered the same problem.

Now, some unexplained oddity is, up to a point, a legitimate device for evoking an atmosphere of strangeness. The author need not explain everything. But, unless the reader is told something definite of what happened, he will feel cheated. He will suspect, often rightly, that the writer thought up all these clever freaks merely to lead him on but did not explain them because he could not think of a plausible explanation. If you leave out an explanation of anything, it should not be because you, the writer, do not know the answer either.

An advantage of the imaginative story is that it is not limited to a stereotyped ending, as is the detective story. The detective story must end with the apprehension of the criminal. Likewise, the love story usually ends with boy getting girl or vice versa. There is a simple historical reason for the ubiquity of the final clinch in love stories. Modern

Western light fiction descends in a fairly straight line from classical Greek comedy. This in turn developed out of primitive vernal fertility rites. These entailed, at least symbolically, a public sexual union in order, in accordance with the laws of sympathetic magic, to encourage the tribal herds and crops to increase.

We have gone beyond that stage today, and readers of imaginative fiction demand neither a happy nor an unhappy ending but simply a logical ending. If it is inevitable in your basic assumptions that boy-robot shall get girl-android, by all means let him have her. If, on the other hand, it is inevitable that mankind shall blow up the earth, let it blow. Some magazines show a slight bias towards one kind of ending or another; but, on the whole, the rule of logical endings, happy or otherwise, can be safely followed in the imaginative field.

☆ ☆ ☆

In addition to the four parts described above, a story also breaks down into shorter natural divisions. Unless a story is very short indeed, there are usually lapses in time. That is, the writer does not keep his searchlight on the action every minute from beginning to end but shifts the scene or takes time out to let his characters eat, sleep, and perform other acts not involved in the story.

In a short story, such a change of scene is usually indicated by a blank space between paragraphs, and sometimes in addition by a large initial letter at the beginning of the new paragraph. In a novelette or novel, the major divisions are indicated by chapters, and these in turn may be broken down into sections as though each were a short story. A very long novel may be further divided, if logic so dictates, into two or three "books," each of which can in turn be subdivided into chapters and sections.

A. E. van Vogt once suggested articulating stories into scenes of 800 words each, by which he meant anything from 600 to 1,000.[6] This means, roughly, two to four pages of manuscript per scene. This is in itself unobjectionable, although we are inclined to let scenes find their natural length. This may range from 100 to 5,000 words, depending upon how much continuous action is called for. If you do not indicate a section division for many pages, a magazine editor is likely to insert a few such divisions arbitrarily into the long, unbroken stretches to give his pages a variegated appearance. This does not harm the story; but an editor may, on the other hand, omit a division that you have indicated, thus baffling the reader when he comes to a sudden shift of time and place without warning.

Most book publishers like chapter titles to list on the contents page, while most magazine publishers prefer chapter numbers only, although both rules have exceptions. We suggest that you insert chapter titles only in a novel intended for book publication. Chapter titles follow the same rules as story titles. Do not make them either too cryptic or too revealing.

There are two ways of dividing a novel into chapters. One is to make the breaks at the natural points—that is, where there is a major change of scene or lapse of time. The other is to make the break at a point of crisis or suspense, as in an old-fashioned serial movie. The latter is the familiar "cliff hanger." While this may seem a childish device to lead the reader on, it can be quite effective, especially in stories wherein suspense or mystery plays a large part.

Burroughs used a simple but effective technique: he would have two stories running simultaneously. Suppose Deja Thoris, his Martian heroine, is about to be put to base uses by the Things that have kidnapped her, while her husband John Carter is frantically searching for her. Burroughs follows Deja until she is about to suffer death or a fate worse than; then he shifts to John and follows him until he is menaced by a similar doom; then back to Deja.

Magazine editors like a cliff hanger, because it enables them to break a serial at a point of crisis to lure the readers back to next month's issue. If you sell one of them a serial, he will write you saying that he will run the story in so many instalments and break it at such-and-such points, and will you please write a set of synopses to precede the second and later instalments? He does not pay extra for this.

☆ ☆ ☆

What point of view shall the author take, or in what person

shall he tell the story? Nearly all stories are told either in the first or in the third person. There have been a couple of stories written in the second person (that is, telling that "you" did this and that) but these are tours-de-force of no great use as models.

If the story is told in the first person, it can be told either by the main character or by an onlooker. The latter is a commonplace of detective stories, Dr. John Watson being the classical detective's stooge-narrator.

Having the hero tell the story gives an effect of intimacy and puts the reader right into the middle of things. But it has a drawback: in a story of dramatic action, it takes the edge off the suspense by assuring the reader that the narrator at least survived to tell the tale. Of course, you can end the story with the narrator's explaining that he was killed, and this is his ghost speaking. But this, too, has been done and is likely to irritate the reader almost as much as the ending in which the narrator explains that it was all a dream.

Although putting the story into the mouth of an onlooker to some extent avoids this peril, it has the disadvantage that the onlooker-narrator cannot be on hand to note all the important incidents and conversations. The hero, for instance, is unlikely to make love to his beloved in the stooge's presence.

First-person stories appeal to the young writer because they are easy to write. They also have an inherent plausibility, because most accounts of real events are in the form of first-person narratives, in which someone tells of his experiences. Their disadvantages, however, are so serious that it is probably best to avoid them unless there is a specific reason, inherent in the story, for using this method. Some editors dislike first-person stories.

If you use the first person, your narrator must say only what a man of his assumed personality, origin, class, education, outlook, and status would actually say. He cannot know anything that such a person would not in fact know, and he cannot use expressions foreign to such a person. A beginner once showed us the manuscript of a story told in the first person by a boxing promoter. This was supposed to be a tough, ill-educated man, yet on the first page he broke into a fancy literary figure of speech.

If a story is told in the third person, it can be told either providentially—that is, as by God or an omniscient writer—or from the point of view of a particular character or characters. The latter is more plausible but means that you must observe the same restrictions as those of the preceding paragraph. The rule is not so rigid in this case. If, however, while following the action through the eyes of Southeast Jones, you suddenly make some general remark that gives the reader information beyond Jones's ken, you have jumped out of Jones's mind and are hovering godlike above the scene.

A good rule is never to change your point of view within a given scene. The reader has had trains of thought himself and so can imagine himself in the place of Southeast Jones, following Jones's thoughts and perceptions. But he has never jumped from his own mind into another's. Never say, for instance: "They were disappointed to see that the surface of the planet Beelzebub was bare of life." While you can tell what "they" are doing and saying, because your point-of-view character can see and hear them, you cannot tell what "they" are thinking without implausibly leaping from mind to mind.

You may either stick to one point of view throughout the story or change from time to time. If you change, it should not be during one scene, but between scenes or chapters. We suggest sticking to one point of view unless you have a good reason for shifting; as, for instance, you have two stories going at once, and the action takes place so far apart that no one character could cover both.

Sprague de Camp has always been partial to the single point of view, with a few exceptions. He has sometimes found it expedient, for example, to take the providential viewpoint for the first few paragraphs while setting the scene and introducing the leading character, and then leaping into that character's mind and staying there.

Once you are in Southeast Jones's mind, however, see only what he sees. Once having merged with his mind, you may not remark that Jones's mustache is getting gray—unless

Jones is looking in a mirror.

Neither may you switch from the third to the first person (as has sometimes been done) without an adequate explanation, as by presenting the first-person story as a report, letter, or other written narrative. *Dracula* is entirely in the form of letters, diaries, medical journals, phonograph records, and newspaper clippings, skillfully woven together.

Some writers narrate their stories purely in terms of physical action and dialogue, without peeping into their characters' minds at all. Hemingway and Bradbury have made effective use of this technique. It works best on Hemingway's anthropoid characters, who have no minds to speak of, but is of only limited use in fiction of ideas.

Establishing a point of view is sometimes complicated by a "frame"—that is, an introduction wherein somebody explains how the narrative came to be recorded. The frame may take the form of an account of finding a manuscript, or receiving the narrative in some other form, as in Cutcliffe Hyne's *The Lost Continent,* Aldous Huxley's *Ape and Essence,* and Olaf Stapledon's *Last and First Men.*

Although a frame may lend plausibility, it makes it harder for the reader to lose himself in the sweep of the narrative. He must get through, not one opening of the story, but two. Frames are seldom used nowadays, because imaginative fiction is so well known that the author need not apologize for straining his reader's credulity.

☆ ☆ ☆

A story has a more or less natural length. It should be long enough to permit you to expound all your basic ideas, narrate the essential events, and explore the effects implicit in your assumptions without writing a single unnecessary word. In practice, the length of a story allows some leeway.

A short story and a novel, while treated in the same way in matters of style, point of view, and subject matter, differ in other respects. In a short story, there is no space to waste. The reader has no tolerance for long beginnings. To hook the reader, shoot the sheriff in the first paragraph. There is no space for great complications and no time for lengthy processes, such as a basic change in a person's character. You cannot develop character; you can at best reveal it and show its relationship to the action. You have a brief development leading up to one major incident, told in a concentrated, concise manner. If you can put in a snapper ending, so much the better.

In a novel, on the other hand, there is time to develop characters. It makes the story better yet if the characters can be shown as changing for better or for worse as they interact with the physical events. You can bring in large ideas and long-drawn-out events. You can depict such massive concepts as galactic empires and the histories of eras. You can devise many complications.

Men of letters sometimes speak of "plot and counterplot" as characteristic of the novel. They mean that, in a long story, it is useful not only to follow one straight line of action but also to bring in subordinate threads of events as well, interwoven with and reacting against the main plot thread. Thus a story might concern itself with the threat of atomic war and the forces pushing for and against it, while the counterplot might be the love story of the chief character. A counterplot is justified if, and only if, it can be so integrated with the main plot that it seems not only natural but also inevitable. It must never be dragged in solely to complicate the plot or to provide a love interest. The reader is easily enough confused without the writer's going out of his way to baffle him.

A novelette is intermediate between a novel and a short story, not only in length but also in techniques. It is the shortest story in which you can undertake an extensive portrayal of character. By the same token, it is the longest in which you can get by without character development. The best course is usually to allow a moderate degree of characterization in such a story—more than in a short story but less than in a novel. Similar advice applies to counterplots and complications.

The writer for imaginative magazines is not rigidly limited in matters of length. While an editor may prefer one length or another, or need stories of a certain length at a given time, most of them welcome a good story of any length from a thousand words up to their limit. If they buy serials, this limit may be as high as 100,000 words. General-circulation magazines, on the other hand, often limit stories to a length such as 5,000 words.

A type of fiction intermediate between a disconnected group of stories and a novel or serial is a series of sequels. We have mentioned the trick of writing several short stories or novelettes about the same character or characters in the same setting. This is one way to get around a magazine's tabu on serials. You can also write a series of connected novels, as Burroughs did with his tales of Tarzan and John Carter.

If you hit upon a character or setting that proves popular, there is no reason for not exploiting it more fully in a series of stories. In such a series, however, there are dangers to avoid.

As soon as you feel that your idea will carry a series, sit down and do some intensive thinking about the background and the over-all history of the period of the stories, the settings, and the characters. Write extensive notes or even a whole pseudo-history, in the form of an essay, as Robert Howard did with his essay "The Hyborian Age." Otherwise, partway through the series, you may have ideas that you cannot use because they are inconsistent with things that you have already written. (Tolkien encountered difficulties of this sort when he expanded the concept of *The Hobbit* into the far larger and more serious *Lord of the Rings.*) You must keep re-reading the earlier stories to avoid inconsistency, for inconsistency is fatal to plausibility.

Some editors take a dim view of stories belonging to a series that a rival editor is publishing. So, if the editor who bought the first two stories of a series bounces the third, your chances of selling this third story elsewhere are less than with a disconnected story.

Lastly, it is hard to keep up the excitement of the first stories of a series. A series tends to run down; unless each story is better than its predecessor, readers may think that it is not even so good. Thus in Sprague de Camp's Johnny Black series, Johnny (his educated bear) started out by saving the world. His achievements dwindled with each story, until in the fourth and last tale he was merely saving his boss's job.

☆ ☆ ☆

Characters are delineated in science fiction and fantasy in much the same way as in other fiction, with some additional complications. Characterization entails hard work but is not so mysterious as it may seem.

The first step in characterization is to visualize your characters as clearly as if they were old friends or acquaintances. Writers often give their characters the personalities of their own kith and kin, although it is prudent to disguise them so that the models shall not recognize themselves. To avoid unpleasantness, they often combine the traits of several real people in one fictional character, as by giving the latter the appearance of one real person, the personality of another, and the speech habits of a third.

Next, write a short biography of each of these characters, covering his life to the time of the story. You need not, however, include his fictitious telephone number, as Sinclair Lewis did. You must know how your character speaks and what he would be likely to do under any given circumstances.

You can help the reader to keep track of the characters by giving them verbal tags. Thus one man may employ pedantic speech, while a second swears, a third stutters, a fourth goes "uh" or "ah," a fifth speaks with an accent, and a sixth constantly says "you see." But tags are at best an aid to characterization, not a substitute for it. They should be applied sparingly, not distorting the character's speech to the point where it becomes hard to read.

Make sure that everything the character does and says in the story is consistent with the attributes you have given him. If, for purposes of the story, he has to act out of character, go back and start over, changing either the character or the events until the latter follow logically from the former.

In real life, a person may sometimes, in an emergency, transcend his limitations of character, as when a timid person risks his life for others. He may even, within limits, perform a physical feat beyond his normal abilities. But no frail, skinny little scholar can really beat up a roughneck twice his size, however much he and the reader might like to see him do so.

SCIENCE FICTION HANDBOOK, REVISED

And once a moron, always a moron; if a character has been portrayed as stupid, he should not suddenly solve some abstruse problem. If, in trying to make your character plausible or sympathetic, you have overloaded him with human frailties, such as laziness, cowardice, or drunkenness, his later accomplishment of some worthy and difficult deed will be flatly incredible.

This is but another case of the principle already mentioned: that, to make a story convincing, you must have scrupulous internal consistency. This applies even more to an imaginative than to a realistic story. As another case of damaging inconsistency, consider Stapledon's *Odd John*. The mutants, having killed a number of ordinary human beings to insure the secrecy of their project, establish a utopian colony on a South Pacific island. In time they are discovered by "normal" men. Suspicious, governments send ships to investigate. But, although the mutants have been portrayed as vastly superior to *Homo sapiens* in intelligence, foresight, and wisdom, they now show little evidence of these powers and passively await their doom.

A character must also be credible. Real heroes and villains are not completely different; real heroes have flaws and real villains, virtues. The old snow-white hero and coal-black villain are no longer so useful as forty years ago. A perfect hero is as unconvincing as a "hero" who is a weak, witless, ineffectual twerp.

To make a character believable, you must build him up as if he were a real person, not a stock type. We all know the character stereotypes: the funny Irishman, the bluff old sea dog, and so forth. In real life, not all Irishmen are funny, not all Scots are thrifty, not all Scandinavians are brave, blue-eyed six-footers, not all sea captains are bluff, not all Orientals are subtle, not all colonels are stupid martinets, and so on.

You are, we hope, sophisticated enough about human character to know that there is little relationship between personality and appearance. There is no such thing as a "cruel mouth" or a "weak chin."

While a character can be expected to change in the course

[120]

of a novel, people do not change overnight without good reason, such as terrible hardship or brain injury. Hence the reformation of the hero in the novel *Gravy Planet,* by Kornbluth and Pohl, is unconvincing. Mitchell Courtenay, a member of the ruling class of advertising agents, has been shown as a slick, selfish, unscrupulous, brutal heel. We do not for a minute believe that his mere conversion to the ideals of the outlawed Conservationists would revolutionize his character; he would likely have been almost as slick, selfish, and so on as a Conservationist as he was as a huckster.

One of the hardest tasks that a fiction writer can set himself is to write an interesting story about a dull, petty character. So beware of making your hero too "average" or "typical."

Extraterrestrial characters are worked out in the same way as human characters, even if one assumes that their personalities differ basically from those of human beings. You must know the aliens' backgrounds, culture, motivations, and individual histories. These may or may not be like those of human beings; the choice is up to you.

You reveal your character's character, not by describing it point by point, but by showing the character acting in accordance with it. Hence you should not write: "Southeast Jones was hard to get along with—selfish and inconsiderate, caring for little but his own convenience and comfort. Moreover, he was so violently choleric that, when he lost his temper over some fancied wrong, we feared he would die of apoplexy."

Do not tell them; show them: "Purpling, Southeast Jones hurled his plate to the floor and screamed at the trembling cook: 'You son of a bitch, you've burned my toast again!' " The reader has learned just as much about Jones in half as many words and has a picture of Jones in action as well.

As a horrible example, in "Lord Mountdrago,"[7] Somerset Maugham introduces his central character by telling the reader: "Lord Mountdrago had many good qualities. He had intelligence and industry. He was widely traveled and spoke several languages fluently. From early youth he had specialized in foreign affairs. . . ." After a page, Maugham gets to Mountdrago's faults: "He was a fearful snob. . . . He was coldly insolent to those whom he looked upon as his social inferiors. He was rude to his servants and insulting to his secretaries. . ." and so on for another full page. While you end up with a vivid picture of Lord Mountdrago, the story stands still during this exposition, like a motion picture that has been halted while somebody steps in front of the screen to explain something.

Since you must economize on words, you cannot let Southeast Jones throw his plate on the floor merely to demonstrate his character. The incident should play a definite part in the development of the story. The causes should be such that Jones inevitably had his outburst just then, and the results should be such that the outcome of the tale would be different if he had not. If you find it hard to make every incident both illustrate character and carry the story forward to its inevitable conclusion—well, did we ever say that writing was an easy way to make a living?

When a character acts as such a character would probably have acted under given circumstances, we say that he was properly motivated. If not, the author has been guilty of false motivation. Nobody does anything for no reason. A man's acts may be a simple, reflexive response to a physical stimulus like hunger or pain, or they may be the outcome of a rational, calculated plan, or they may be caused by some buried psychological urge. But there must be some reason. It is up to the writer to see that everything his main characters do is accounted for by plausible motivating forces. If a character suddenly fails to respond as he normally would to the given motivations, the reader's illusion is strained.

Let us give an example of false motivation. In his earliest novel, *The Mightiest Machine*, John Campbell takes his explorers to a distant planet, where they meet a race of satyrs or goat-men. These, it transpires, came from earth in the days of Lemuria. As soon as the heroes see these beings, they are seized with a violent "instinctive" hatred of them. As the satyrs feel the same way about men, nothing will serve but a war of extermination. But human beings have no "instinctive" hatreds; they hate only what they have been taught to hate.

Edmond Hamilton likewise erred in his *City at World's End.* He attributed to small-town Americans, tossed into the remote future, hysterical excitement at the sight of an intelligent extraterrestrial, even though they have had hints of its presence, and fanatical determination not to leave the earth, even though with the death of the sun, the earth has become barren and useless.

If a character belongs to some well-defined class of people, such as capitalists or scientists, it is well for the writer to study people of that class before trying to portray a "typical" member. Otherwise, the character emerges as a cardboard stereotype with little reality. Thus Duncan H. Munro, in his Arabian Nights romp "Hell's Bells," places his hero in contemporary London and provides him with a companion: a comic-strip silly-ass Englishman, in complete morning garb from top hat and monocle to purple spats, talking the upper-class British slang of fifty to two hundred years ago: "Begad, sir!" and the like. Such a person would be almost as outré in modern London as in Terre Haute.

If your cast includes children, it would be wise to make sure that they speak and act as children of their age really do. In her fantasy "The Bird," Margaret St. Clair impaired her illusion by describing a child as eleven years old and then having him act as if he were five.

Each main character should be adequately characterized during his first appearance on the stage. He can be characterized not only through his own actions but also by being seen through the eyes of other characters and by the impression he makes upon them.

☆ ☆ ☆

The number of main characters in a story should be the smallest that the writer can manage with and still account for all the events. You need not characterize everybody in the story—least of all when the tale takes place in urban surroundings, through which many people pass briefly. If you fully characterize a dozen or more, the reader may have trouble keeping track of them. Schuyler Miller and Sprague de Camp erred in their early novel *Genus Homo* by trying to

[123]

characterize all twenty-odd human beings in their cast. They would have done better to concentrate on the leading half-dozen and let the rest be lay figures.

It is artistically bad to have two characters who duplicate each other's function in the story. So do not bring in two ghosts (like Horace Walpole), or two mad scientists, or two Alpha Centaurian emperors.

Try to bring in all the important characters early in the story, not all at once but in fairly quick succession. If the exigencies of the plot require that an important character appear for the first time towards the end, he should be so foreshadowed that the reader has a good picture of him when he does appear.

Struggling young writers have a weakness for making their heroes struggling young writers like themselves. This follows the principle of writing what you know best, but it is a narcissistic tendency and makes the story seem amateurish. Avoid it. It has been done to death. Besides, writers are not, on the whole, such appealing fictional subjects as people of other kinds.

☆ ☆ ☆

Give your characters definite names. To call them simply "the chief" or "the investigator," as Taine did in "Tomorrow," is confusing. Give male characters masculine names and female characters feminine names. Girls named "Cameron" or "Storm" are only a source of bewilderment to the reader. Grown men are usually alluded to by surname ("Jones"), women by full name ("Clarissa MacDougall" or "Mrs. Kinnison") or by given name only.

Do not give all your characters commonplace Anglo-Saxon names of similar sound and length. C. S. Lewis named his interplanetary hero and villain Ransom and Weston, but the names are so much alike that it is hard to remember which is which. On the other hand, do not give them all queer names like "Theophilus Pancake." Give some short names and some long, some common and some unusual, as they actually occur in any random group of people. Make sure that there are no near-duplicates like Jones and Johnson, or Aker and Baker. Do not use symbolic names like "Ernest Everhard," the bull-necked proletarian hero of London's *Iron Heel,* or patently artificial names like "Nosnibor" ("Robinson" backwards) as Butler did in *Erewhon.*

Non-Anglo-Saxon readers object to some writers' habit of blandly assuming that the future galactic civilization will be an exclusively Anglo-Saxon affair and that all the officers of the Interstellar Constabulary will hence have names like Green and Wilson and Carpenter. While this probably does no harm in stories for the juvenile trade, it is a legitimate criticism.

Sprague de Camp tries to give names to his characters in the proportions that would occur among real people under his basic assumptions. For instance, if he were telling of a British expedition to Mars in the year 2000, the names would be nearly all British (Anglo-Saxon and Celtic). If it were an American expedition at that time, the names would be half to two-thirds British, the next largest group German, and smaller proportions of other nationalities, because that is how names occur in the United States. If he were telling of an interstellar expedition of 2500, there would probably be many Asiatic and some African names as well as names of European origin.

That brings us to the problem of naming places and people in exotic settings such as the remote past, the remote future, or another world.

Obviously it will not do to choose names like Jones and Schmidt, Chicago and Berlin. One can make up simple nonsense-syllables like "Ba" and "Gu," but these are unconvincing because real languages are not like that. There would not be enough syllables to go round. Also, the reader would have trouble telling these names apart.

One can adopt names from Terran history and mythology. But if the reader comes across "Rhiannon" as a name for a man or a planet (as Leigh Brackett has used it), it knocks a hole in his suspension-of-disbelief if he happens to know that Rhiannon was an ancient Welsh goddess.

Sprague de Camp's system is to invent an exotic language with logical grammar and phonology, modeled after some Terran tongue. Gozashtandou in his Krishna stories is a kind of pig-Persian, while Avtinyk in *Rogue Queen* is pig-Welsh. The writer must not, however, let his linguistic enthusiasm lead him to give names too long or too difficult or too full of diacritical marks.

One modern system of teaching children to read causes difficulty in this matter. "Sight reading" treats words as units to be recognized by over-all shape, like Chinese ideographs, without bothering about the sound meaning of individual letters. Some children learn to read faster by this method but never master the vagaries of English spelling. When they meet a word of unfamiliar shape, it baffles them. It may help to give them a pronunciation guide at the beginning of the story; but this will not help much, because many view such a list as hard work.

The best that one can do is to concoct names belonging to a more or less consistent phonetic scheme and not individually difficult. So do not bestow on any character a name like Xyczphthûsz. At the same time, names should differ among themselves enough to avoid confusion. See that no two leading characters have names beginning with the same letter.

☆ ☆ ☆

Finally, let us consider the main types of story and point out which are the more promising for new writers.

Many have classified imaginative stories. Heinlein divided stories on a basis of interest into gadget stories and human-interest stories. He then further subdivided the latter group into three types of plot: Boy-meets-Girl, the Little Tailor, and the Man Who Learned Better.[8]

The first of these is one of the oldest types of story but still good. All sorts of variations are possible. For instance, in Heinlein's *Methuselah's Children,* the long-lived hero is confronted with the problem of whether to marry his great-great-great-great-granddaughter. Genetically, their relationship is negligible, but such a union still seems somehow incestuous. In Philip José Farmer's "The Lovers," the hero learns that his sweetheart is descended from insectlike organisms that mimic the human female. A motion-picture editor has been quoted as saying that Hollywood's new, science-fictional version of the traditional formula is: Boy-meets-Girl, Boy-loses-Girl, Boy-*builds*-Girl.[9] This almost fits the plot of del Rey's "Helen O'Loy."

What is not needed in imaginative stories is a conventional love interest, in the form of a professor's beautiful daughter, arbitrarily dragged into a story to which she is irrelevant, solely to provide love interest. Neither, on the other hand, need any legitimate element of love or sex be arbitrarily excluded on the assumption that most readers are maladjusted boys who do not wish to hear about such things. Use love and sex if they logically belong but not otherwise.

The Little Tailor refers to stories of success or failure: the little shot who becomes a big shot or vice versa. The Man Who Learned Better is the hero who starts out with one point of view but has another imposed upon him by experience. Many stories fall into two or more classes at once.

The classification—out of an infinite possible number—that we favor groups stories according to the main point of interest. We like to classify them as stories of the exotic, of the incongruous, of a discovery, of an invention, or of a major change.

Stories of the exotic depict a strange world. This world may be in the remote past, or in the future, or on another planet, or in another "dimension." In stories of the incongruous, the appeal centers upon the contrast between such an environment, or a being from it, and a familiar one, whether the contrast be provided by an earthman on the planet Krishna or a Krishnan on earth. In stories of discovery, the discovery may be in space, as in tales of planetary exploration, or in scientific knowledge. Stories of invention are self-explanatory; while in stories of a major change, the change may be caused by man's own actions (war, overpopulation, or plain folly) or by some vast catastrophe.

Let us run over a few of the established types of story and point out certain limitations or possibilities of these themes. First, there are stories laid in another time. The future has always been good and, as far as we can see, will go on being good indefinitely. Events keep happening in the real world to provide data on which to build more pictures of possible futures. Thus the atomic bomb of 1945 made nearly all

[127]

previous stories about future war obsolete but provided the basis for a whole new cycle. Beware, however, of setting a story only a few years, or even a couple of decades, in the future. Before you know it, that time will have arrived. Then your story will become dated by events and its reprint value impaired.

You may either lay your story in the future or move a character from the present into the future. But the old "Sleeper" plot, which goes back to a legend about the long-dormant Cretan poet Epimenedes, has been done to death. Throwing the hero forward by time machine is not much fresher. Altogether, there seems little reason for not simply setting the scene in your imagined future and playing it straight.

Science-fiction and fantasy stories laid in the past face certain problems. Those laid in historical periods are not imaginative unless they introduce definite imaginative elements, such as supernatural beings or intruders into the historical milieu from other worlds or times. While many such stories have been written, the field still has wide possibilities, because most of the existing stories have been confined to a few well-known periods like Imperial Rome and often give a superficial and inaccurate picture of the setting, whatever period is chosen.

Stories laid in prehistoric lands or on lost continents are a good choice. The facts of human prehistory, while fairly clear to archaeologists, are not well enough known to laymen to spoil such yarns. Such stories have, however, but a limited market. Stories of cave men who discover things have often been done, sometimes well and sometimes badly. It strains the illusion to make the same man discover fire, the bow, the canoe, and monogamy all in one lifetime, when in fact such discoveries were strung out over hundreds of thousands of years. And the writer should know better than to mix his cave men with dinosaurs, which, in the days of the cave men, had been extinct for over sixty million years.

Stories laid in the here-and-now will continue popular. The time assumed by most such stories should not be exactly the present, but the immediate future, too near for our present environment to have appreciably changed but distant enough so that the reader would not expect to find the events narrated in tomorrow's newspaper. If the story takes place in 1975 or earlier, the writer must resort to some ruse, such as destroying the evidence, to make plausible the fact that the story is not already known.

Stories can be laid on other worlds or in one of those other frames of reference or space-time continua sometimes called "dimensions" or "planes." Such stories can be laid in any time—past, present, future, or indeterminate.

If you wish to lay your yarn on a planet of our solar system, consider what sort of Mars and Venus you wish to use. The Mars and Venus of Burroughs, Moore, Bradbury, and Brackett were fine places for romantic adventures, but the astronautical discoveries of recent decades have made them as implausible as the moon of Cyrano de Bergerac. Encumbered with one of the protective suits that we now know to be necessary in such places, the hero would find it awkward to rescue a princess from a wicked high priest and even more so to make love to her afterwards, and the princess herself becomes more improbable with each new discovery. These difficulties apply *a fortiori* to other solar planets like Mercury and Jupiter.

One can move out to the other stars, as there is reason to suspect that, probably, millions of them are equipped with planets. If, however, you mean to shoot people to such stars and back within the span of a normal human lifetime, you must cope with the problem of distance. Even the nearest stars are several light-years away, and the more distant visible ones hundreds of light-years. There is a well-grounded principle of physics that keeps things from going faster than light. Writers have used several solutions: putting their spacemen to sleep during their long trip; flying them so fast that, in accordance with the Lorenz-Fitzgerald contraction, time slows down for them; making the space ship a home for successive generations; or slipping the ship into a whatnot called "hyperspace" and getting them there in minutes. The last solution makes the story a quasi-fantasy, but no more so than a backwards time-travel tale.

There is still a wide-open field for stories laid on other planets, either planets of other stars or worlds in other continua, where life has evolved somewhat differently from that on earth.

Among stories laid in the present, one must select with care. The old lost-race theme, which reached a climax in the novels of Haggard and Merritt, is worn out because practically all the earth's surface has now been explored or at least flown over, so that there is no plausible place left where lost cities or dinosaurs might survive. The hollow earth (besides its physical impossibility) and the Atlanteans living under glass domes at the bottom of the sea have both been pretty well exploited.

For contrasting different eras, time travel still has vitality, and the readers do not seem to mind the built-in paradox.

Exploration of other worlds, although the subject of a multitude of stories, shows no sign of exhaustion. But the writer cannot simply toss his explorers on some planet solely to have them look at the quaint animals or be attacked by the natives and rescued at the last minute. The story should have more thought content. It can deal with the psychological hazards of exploration, the contrasts between human and alien cultural patterns, or the difficulty of establishing a *modus vivendi* with beings of different organization. Cultural relativity is an excellent subject, but you should learn about real cultural patterns before tackling a story of ethnographic speculation.

Similar advice applies to stories of exploration of other continua. One sub-type is the tale of alternate universes, which might have existed if, say, Napoleon had won Waterloo or the Norse had successfully colonized America.

The story of extraterrestrial visitors has been good ever since Voltaire's "Micromegas" and will continue so for a long time. But the flying-saucer craze has been overworked, as once were the countless stories wherein extraterrestrials had conquered earth and oppressed earthmen were trying to oust them. The conquest of the earth would be much harder now than when Wells wrote *The War of the Worlds*.

The story of atomic doom was run into the ground in the

years following Hiroshima, so that a reaction by the readers against it set in. The theme is probably destined for a long life, however, because it refers to a real and pressing problem. There have been many stories in which mankind was almost wiped out by atomic war, disease, or other catastrophe, and the survivors struggle back from barbarism. If you use the theme of Our Barbarous Descendants, try to find some new angles in causes, development, or outcome.

There is a wide field for stories of technological problems, such as Raymond F. Jones's "Production Test," about a problem in the manufacture of space suits. But the writer should know something of the engineering involved; a mere account of a technical or manufacturing process is not a story.

An even broader scope is afforded by stories dealing with human problems arising from scientific and technological advances: medical discoveries, overpopulation, exhaustion of resources, degenerative mutation pressure, and so on. Only a fraction of this field has been exploited.

Many stories have been written about biological innovations: mutations (either towards supermen or towards monsters), robots and androids, and giant mechanical brains. But many more remain to be written. The mere idea of the "revolt of the robots," however, has been overdone ever since Capek's *R.U.R.*

In stories about animal mutations, do not expand insects to the size of horses or whales. It does not work, because of the square-cube law. When we double the insect's dimensions, we increase his strength and the area of his breathing apparatus by four but multiply his mass by eight. Hence we cannot enlarge him very much before he can no longer move or breathe.

There remains the field of pure or supernatural fantasy. Although fantasy has commercial limitations, because the market is smaller than for straight science fiction, some authors are at their best in stories of this kind. Some cannot work up interest in fiction of any other type. Even successful science-fiction writers often like to write an occasional fantasy for a change. Some areas of fantasy have not been well exploited.

The common ghost story, one of the oldest kinds of imaginative tale, has been so thoroughly worked over, ever since the witch of Endor brought up the spirit of the prophet Samuel, that one needs an idea of exceptional originality and power before undertaking a ghost story. The same applies to stories of werewolves and vampires. There is no point in adding one more tired tale of shooting the werewolf with a silver bullet to the mountainous pile that already exists.

That, however, still leaves a great gaggle of spirits, fairies, angels, demons, witches, wizards, alchemists, and magical spells to choose from. If you wish to use one of the old mythologies, we suggest avoiding those of ancient Greece and pagan Scandinavia. Zeus, Odin, and their colleagues have been put to work many a time and oft, while many other pantheons—Egyptian, Babylonian, Iranian, Hindu, and so on—have had little attention.

In the 1960's, the success of Tolkien's *Lord of the Rings* and of the Conan stories by Robert Howard and his posthumous colleagues caused a notable surge in the popularity of the heroic fantasy, or sword-and-sorcery fiction. Some of the heroic stories, such as those of Fritz Leiber and the late David Mason, were good; others were less distinguished. Some really bad ones discouraged interest in the genre. Heroic fantasy may continue to have its ups and downs for a long time to come. For those who want to write stories of this kind, we suggest that they use plots more original than the simple one of the big barbarian oaf who slaughters monsters, wicked wizards, and decadent civilized scoundrels with equal ease. Howard could get away with this simple scheme because he had a knack of storytelling that few can match today.

Having prepared for writing an imaginative story, by deciding what kind to write, conceiving a basic idea, and plotting a tale, let us now put paper into typewriter and get going.

WRITING

AN IMAGINATIVE STORY

For a writer, there is no substitute for applying the seat of the pants to the seat of the chair and putting down one word after another. Sometimes, a writer who has—or thinks he has—all the necessary equipment and ideas finds that he gets stuck. The words refuse to come.

The usual explanation is that he is not yet ready to write the story. He has nothing much to say, or what he has to say has not been adequately planned and organized. At times, a writer may have overwhelming personal problems that induce a state of nerves. Or, his story may have "frozen" before it was in a sufficiently entertaining form, as if his unconscious had made up its mind that the story had to be this way and no other. In such cases, the writer can only put the story away and start another.

A crucial part of any story is the opening. The opening locates the reader in time and space and informs him what is happening to whom. It should introduce the leading characters, name them, and characterize them concisely but accurately, thus:

> Two minutes before he disappeared forever from
> the Earth he knew, Joseph Schwartz strolled along
> the pleasant streets of suburban Chicago quoting
> Browning to himself.[1]

In this paragraph, you have an answer to the questions of who, where, and what sort of person. The next few sentences tell more about Schwartz (a retired tailor born in Europe) and identify the time of the story (now). To make sure that the reader gets the name of the leading character right, it is not uncommon to place his name first in the story:

> Dirk Barnevelt hunched his moose-like form over his typewriter and wrote.[2]

The opening also sets the tone of the story. When you read the following passage, you know that you are starting a story of broad humor:

> When Quintus Bland set out to enjoy the evening, he had not the vaguest idea that he was destined to become a skeleton. Yet that is exactly what he did become—an impressive structure composed entirely of bone as far as the eye could reach.[3]

On the other hand, an opening of the following type tells the reader that he can expect a tense, serious story of atomic research or power:

> "Put down that wrench!"
>
> The man addressed turned slowly around and faced the speaker. His expression was hidden by a grotesque helmet, part of a heavy, lead-and-chromium armor which shielded his entire body, but the tone of voice in which he answered showed nervous exasperation.
>
> "What the hell's eating you, doc?" He made no move to replace the tool in question.[4]

It is not playing fair with the reader to start off on one tone and then shift to another. Kuttner did this in "A Gnome There Was." This tale begins as a jolly fantastic romp and then at the end, quite suddenly and for no special reason, condemns the hero to a horrible fate. Such a shift in tone makes the reader resentful, as if somebody had pulled a chair out from under him. The same applies to stories that end with the hero's awakening and learning that it was all a dream.

The opening should also contain a "narrative hook" to titillate the reader's interest. The hook may be some incongruity or some striking element of the story. It may foreshadow events to come or give the reader a taste of swift movement or excitement. Several of the openings already quoted contain obvious narrative hooks. Except in Gothic revival novels, we cannot nowadays start off with the Victorian cliché: "Had I but known what dread fate awaited me as I entered that sinister portal. . . ." This technique was worn out years ago, but a more subtle hint of things to come is not out of place. One of Sprague's narrative hooks was:

> The broad Hudson, blue under spring skies, was dotted with sails. The orchards in the valley were aglow with white and purple blossoms. Beyond the river frowned Storm King, not much of a mountain by western standards, but impressive enough to a York Stater. The landscape blazed with the vivid green of young leaves—and Sir Howard van Slyck, second son of the Duke of Poughkeepsie, wished to God he could get at the itch under his breastplate without going to the extreme of dismounting and removing half his armor.[5]

Naturally, the author hoped that the reader would be so curious as to what armored knights and dukes were doing in the Hudson Valley that nothing would prevent him from reading on.

The opening should also begin the *movement* of the story. In fiction, movement may be physical action, such as Joseph Schwartz's strolling or Dirk Barnevelt's typing. It may be dialogue, as between Heinlein's atomic-plant workers. It may be merely mental movement as in the case of Sir Howard's train of thought.

But something must happen, something related to the story as a whole. To spend the first few pages in static description, without any action, is fatal. And the shorter the story, the less time you have to fool around before the actual events begin. The three and a half sentences of pure description that precede Sir Howard's reflections are about as much as any writer should dare to use at the start, though some writers do use more. If Sprague were to write that story today, he would probably mention Sir Howard's itch even sooner. "Shoot the sheriff on the first page" is a good rule, especially in action stories.

☆ ☆ ☆

Having devised a powerful opening, the writer narrates the various incidents that lead up to the climax and denouement, scene by scene. Each scene must delineate the main characters, trace the changes that take place in their status and condition, show the relationships between them, and prepare the reader for the scenes to come. Difficult? Certainly. Fiction-writing is not an easy profession.

In a well-built story, each incident is put in for a good reason. Each incident carries the story along towards its end and is never introduced solely for effect, or to expound the writer's beliefs, or to indulge his prejudices and dislikes, or to fill space. Writers of the cruder forms of space opera may have their hero and heroine marooned on a strange planet and chivvied by monsters solely because they think their readers like heroes saving heroines from monsters. Monsters are good in imaginative fiction, but they are much better if they can be integrated into the structure of the story.

In the development of a story, it is a grave mistake to "legislate yourself out of trouble"—to employ the long arm of coincidence, the opportune accident, or some conveniently discovered fact, hitherto undisclosed, to get your hero out of a hopeless predicament. Of course, there are plenty of accidents in real life, sometimes fortunate, more often disastrous. Therefore, it is legitimate to let accidents play a part in the story, but only to set up the problem, not to solve it.

For instance, it is legitimate to have the space ship *John W. Campbell* crippled by a meteor at the start of a story that deals with the forced landing of the ship on a strange planet and the struggle of her people to survive. But it does not satisfy the reader if, at the end of the story, just as our characters have by heroic efforts escaped from their space-shipwreck, another meteor annihilates them.

Young writers sometimes commit this kind of fictional mayhem, not to entertain the reader but to show what devilishly clever, superior, cynical, ironic fellows they are—fellows who really grasp the blind hostility of the universe. Such writers merely annoy the reader, who already knows about the blind hostility of the universe and wants a story in which the actions of the people bear some causal relation to the outcome.

Likewise, avoid such illegitimate and unconvincing expedients as having an intelligent character fall into a state of temporary stupidity, not because he has been drugged or dropped on his head, but because the writer wishes to entangle him in some plot element. This literary cretinism commonly afflicts the fictional scientist who refuses to consider some plain piece of evidence contrary to his established beliefs; the hero who falls into traps that would not deceive a twelve-year-old; and the villain who gets the drop on the hero and then instead of blowing his head off stands taunting him and boasting of his sins until the space marines arrive.

Sometimes you find yourself confronted with a scene that is essential to the story but that for one reason or another—inexperience, ignorance, embarrassment, emotional involvement—you are disinclined to write. The professional does not duck an obligatory scene, as by skipping over it with a brief summary. The thought of writing a love scene may appall you because you lack amatory experience; but if such a scene is essential to the story, either write it anyway or get another story.

☆ ☆ ☆

A story involves action, not static description. If you read a story carefully, you will note that sentences are of two kinds: those which are purely descriptive and expository, such as "The broad Hudson, blue under spring skies, was dotted with sails," and those in which something happens, such as "The man addressed turned slowly around and faced the speaker."

During a sentence of the former kind, the story stands still; during the latter, it moves. The larger the proportion of action sentences, the more swiftly the story moves and the better the reader likes it. A mass of straight description in a story kills the reader's interest.

Still, in an imaginative story, which by definition contains unfamiliar elements, the writer cannot present a narrative with no explanation or description at all. The reader will not know what the author is talking about.

This dilemma can be solved in several ways. The most convenient is to present description disguised as action or dialogue. Thus one might have written: "Sir Howard van Slyck gazed across the broad Hudson, blue under spring skies and dotted with sails." He would have conveyed the same information but given it the illusion of action by having Sir Howard perform the act of gazing. For more extensive description, the writer can have his protagonist travel about his imaginary setting, seeing one thing after another.

Description can also be worked into dialogue. One character can tell another the things the reader must know. But, while such dialogical descriptions may be necessary to a story, they are not a substitute for a story. Therefore, they should be held to a minimum.

The best system is so to integrate your story that the physical details all play an active part in the tale. For example, in Sprague's novel *The Glory That Was,* the hero pays several visits to the Acropolis of Athens in the time of Pericles. On the first visit, the writer described several statues, temples, and other ornaments that stood on the site at that date. But he did not bring in one statue for its own sake. Every one played an active rôle in the story, then or later.

You may find that a certain amount of exposition, description, and summary are unavoidable. In that case, give it, but make it as easy as possible for the reader by writing as smoothly and clearly as you can, even using such petty tricks as rhythmic or alliterative prose, or tossing in some foreshadowing remark to lure the reader on. Once, at the beginning of a novelette, one author had occasion to introduce some rather uninteresting geographical and future-historical data; so, to carry the reader along, he began with an obvious narrative hook:

> Claude Godwin became involved with the naked princess as follows:
>
> In driving north from Santa Barbara most people follow Route US 101, which cuts inland across the base of Point Conception. . . .[6]

While all sentences narrating an action may be said to move, some move faster than others. Those that move the fastest have a simple structure of substantives and verbs with the necessary prepositions, conjunctions, and other operative words to tie them together. Those that move slowly are stuffed with adjectives and adverbs.

Adjectivitis is a common fault of tyronic writers, who might write: "a brutal-looking, short-necked, thick-bodied, bestially hairy man with long dangling arms, short bowed legs, a broad flattened nose, and sinister little eyes scowling under beetling eyebrows. . ." when they could simply say "an apelike man" and let it go at that. If a given piece of writing seems to move slowly, it can often be speeded up by the simple expedient of underlining every adjective and adverb and then deleting half or three-quarters of these modifiers.

When a place or person has once been characterized, it is not necessary to repeat this description every time the object reappears. It is not necessary to repeat it at all, except that you may remind the reader of some outstanding characteristic of a man, such as fatness or baldness, a few times in the story to help him to keep the characters straight.

Nor is it necessary, in describing a character, to go into fine anatomical detail. In the first place, the reader will not remember all the details. In the second, if he is given a few hints, he will fill in the rest with his own mental picture.

Nor should the writer give minute details that have no bearing on the outcome of the story. Thus, if your hero sits down to a meal, you need not tell everything he eats, unless the food has some bearing on the plot—for instance, if he gets sick as a result of the meal, or if he orders a more expensive meal than he can pay for.

☆ ☆ ☆

Nearly all stories contain dialogue—imaginary conversations among the characters. The writer must be particularly careful with dialogue, for unrealistic dialogue can instantly destroy a reader's interest.

Fictional dialogue tries to give the illusion of actual conversation, but it is not a stenographic transcript of real conversation. Most real speech, if recorded verbatim, is insufferably trivial, rambling, repetitious—dull, full of hesitations, irrelevancies, and false starts. The larger part of it (the sort you overhear on the subway or at an afternoon bridge party) consists of boasts: "I says to him: 'So what if you are the boss? You can't talk to me like that!' " or complaints: "I won't stand for it! I don't care if he is my wife's brother-in-law!" or pointless personal anecdotes: "So the dentist said that tooth was impacted, and he'd better take it out, but I said. . . ."

When we ourselves talk like that, our speech does not bore us because we are talking about things of real personal concern. But they would be of no interest to a stranger, and the reader is in the position of a stranger eavesdropping on the story's characters. You can use some of this boresome speech to give atmosphere, but a little of it goes a long way.

For fictional purposes, dialogue is speech from which most of the irrelevancies, hesitations, and repetitions have been pruned away, leaving little beyond those statements that actually bear upon the story. The reader knows this and accepts the convention. Painfully realistic dialogue, which rambles all over the lot before getting to the point, soon becomes tedious.

To retain the illusion of real speech, avoid giving great unbroken paragraphs of discourse, unless the character is actually delivering a lecture and the lecture is germane to the story. It is particularly ill-advised to interrupt a sequence of fast action by long speeches. For example, in Fowler Wright's *The World Below,* the hero, trapped with his amphibian companion in the burning citadel of the Killers, takes time to try, condemn, and kill a group of fellow-captives called Bat-things, of whose moral code he self-righteously disapproves.

Back-and-forth conversation generally consists of short sentences alternating between the speakers, with one interlocutor sometimes uttering a whole paragraph at a time. Hence the successful short-sentence dialogue of Hemingway and Bradbury.

In every dialogue, the reader must know who is making each speech to whom. If there are only two interlocutors, the problem is simple. You identify them at the start and then assume that they alternate as speakers, thus:

"Are they coming yet?" said Kinnison.

"I don't see them," said Gosseyn.

"Well, let me know."

"I will."

"They're likely to sneak in through hyperspace, you know."

"Oh, I never thought of that."

If, however, the conversation continues for half a page or more, one must identify the speakers from time to time, or the reader will lose track of them. Machen had the bad habit of letting dialogues run on for pages without reminding the reader who was saying what.

If the two characters are of the opposite sex, you can use "he said" and "she said." Do not be self-conscious about using the word "said" over and over, because the reader never notices. Do not go out of your way to find odd synonyms for "said." Only a tyro writes:

"I hate you!" she shrieked.

"So what?" he sneered.

"I'll kill you!" she persisted.

"Go ahead," he taunted.

An occasional variation of "said," such as "he answered" or "he shouted," is all right, but avoid such monstrosities as the sample above. Nor should you make frequent use of adverbs to indicate the manner of speaking. This should be evident from the words themselves. Do not write: " 'Oh—really—uh—I didn't know—' she stammered confusedly." Her confusion is obvious, so "she said" is quite sufficient.

If you have more than two interlocutors, you may have to name each of the speakers every time to keep the reader straight, unless your dialogue is nearly all between two of them, the others interjecting only an occasional remark. If you have three or more speakers, do not have them speak in rotation, going round and round the circle, but cause them to speak in the order in which they would be likely to speak according to their respective interest in and knowledge of the subjects discussed.

Everything said in dialogue should as far as possible both characterize the speaker and carry the story forward. Of course, you cannot put much characterization into a simple "yes" or "no," but you should follow this principle as far as possible. Everything said should be in character: no poetic rhapsodies from unpoetic people, and no profound sociological pronouncements from shallow characters who neither know nor care about such matters.

Before writing the final draft, go over the story to see that tags of speech attributed to each character are judiciously distributed throughout the story. If the character is speaking ordinary colloquial English, have him use the usual contractions "it's," "don't," et cetera. He would use forms like "it is," and "do not" only if he were a pedant or a foreigner or were making a formal speech.

Avoid indirect discourse except when it is the only alternative to writing a lot of repetitious or uninteresting speech. Thus you might say: "Southeast Jones spoke for an hour," or "Southeast Jones repeated to the Martian what he had told the Venerian." You would not wish to reproduce a one-hour speech verbatim or to repeat a previous speech.

☆ ☆ ☆

How about dialects and foreign accents? Many writers come a cropper here, either by not knowing the different kinds of sub-standard English (in an early story, Eric Frank Russell caused Americans to misplace their *h's* in the old Cockney manner) or by trying to indicate every departure from a theoretical norm. If dialogue is not a stenographic report of real speech, still less is it a phonetic transcription of a tape recording.

The worst method of indicating dialect is to respell a large proportion of the speaker's words phonetically, as Alexander M. Phillips does in his fantasy *The Mislaid Charm*: "Vorringwoot! Goot! Now, I asg you some quesjuns, und you speakg up qvick und true! I know iv you lie, Vorringwoot, und I'm telling you now you be zorry iv you do!"[7]

Such a speech is more harmful in slowing down the reader than helpful in characterizing the speaker. Although phonetic respelling was common in fiction in the last century, as in Kipling's Indian stories, it is now undesirable, save in very small doses, because readers who have learned sight reading fail to recognize the respelled words at first glance and have to go back to puzzle them out. English is a poor language with which to play spelling games, because its spelling is so ambiguous that even the reader who reads by syllables cannot always tell what sounds the respelled words are trying to indicate.

The best way to indicate dialect is to reproduce such mistakes of word order and word usage as the speaker would commonly make, with perhaps a *very* few respelled words. Here, the speaker is a Dane:

> "That is correct," said the Captain. "I was yust remembering how I am in the city of Boston one St. Patrick's day, walking down the dock and minding my own business. Along comes this big Irishman, and anybody can see he has too much to drink, and because I do not have the green on me for the day, he pushes me. Once is all right, but the second time, I got my little Danish up, and I pushed him in the water—with my fist. But I was really very good to him, because if I had not done this, he would be falling in the water to drown after dark when there is nobody to rescue him."[8]

If you know your speaker's mother tongue, you can translate the speech into it and back, preserving features of grammar and word-order of the foreign language. And you can always simply say that Schmidt spoke with a German accent and let it go at that.

Do not cause a foreign speaker whose English is otherwise good to sprinkle his speech with commonplace expressions in his own tongue. Seabury Quinn's Jules de Grandin, despite all his years of spook-hunting in America, continues to shower his hearers with *oui, non, tiens, mon Dieu, eh bien, hélas, mon vieux, Mademoiselle, ma pauvre* and *sacré bleu*. When a man learns a foreign language, these common expressions are the first things he learns and the ones to which he would be least likely to revert. A foreigner normally falls back on his mother tongue only under stress—when he is astonished, excited, drunk, or dying—or when he does not know an English word and has to ask for help.

Never try to indicate proletarian speech by such respellings as "th' " for "the," "an' " for "and," or " 'f" for "if." These are ordinary forms of these words. Such disguises merely irritate. For the same reason, do not respell "new" as "noo," "what" as "wot," or the British "ask" as "ahsk." These are normal pronunciations over much of the English-speaking world and should not be considered odd or distinctive. Such respellings as "pleez" for "please" or "shure" for "sure," such as one sees in comic-strip balloons, are beneath contempt. How else would you say "please" and "sure"?

How do you represent the speech of a man who is "really" speaking some tongue other than modern English—say Chinese or Old High Martian?

That depends. If you wish to emphasize the similarity of the setting to the modern English-speaking world, or if this language is the only one spoken in the story, use ordinary colloquial English with the contractions "it's," "don't," and the rest. If you wish to emphasize the setting's differences from that of today, or if your characters speak two or more languages and you wish to distinguish among them, you may modify your colloquial English by spelling out the contractions, or by using archaisms or exotic expressions, or by translating some phrases literally—but not to the point where the speech becomes hard to read or distracts the reader from the story.

Suppose that Southeast Jones enters a time-machine, whizzes back to Fourth-Dynasty Egypt, and lands in King Khufu's bedroom just as Pharaoh is turning in after a hard day of pyramid-building. The king accosts our hero, who knows Fourth-Dynasty Egyptian. Khufu could say: "Where did you come from? What's your name?"

Or he might even say: "Whence came you, fellow? What is your name?"

But do not have the Pharaoh burst into Middle English: "Whence camest thou, caitiff churl? How art thou yclept?" Nor yet into some specialized, slangy variety of modern

English: "Say, Mac, what piece of woodwork did you crawl outa, huh?"

If you wish to remind the reader that a character is "really" speaking a foreign language, you can translate some expression literally. As an extreme example, Thorne Smith has a Frenchman say: "Tonight I have of pleasure, but now, my friend, I cut. It is that I trim the garden. He is in disarray. Me, I shall introduce order and make all things fair. Regard! I clip, is it not?"[9]

That is all right in Thornesmithian farce-comedy, where anything goes for a laugh. But for a more serious work it would be too broad; one or two Gallicisms in the paragraph would be plenty.

Or, you may have your character speak a word or two in his own tongue. This should be done very sparingly, and in cases where either the meaning of the word is obvious or it does not matter whether the reader understands it or not.

For instance in *The Glory That Was,* two English-speaking men of the twenty-seventh century, yachting in the Mediterranean, land in the Piraeus in Greece at night and find themselves in what seem to be Classical Greek surroundings. When they are attacked by thieves, another man helps to drive the thieves off. They speak. We are seeing the action through the eyes of the hero, Bulnes, who knows several modern languages, including a smattering of modern Greek, but does not know Classical Greek, which the stranger is speaking. Bulnes' companion, Flin, does know Classical Greek, so the conversation goes:

> *"Chairē!"* said the newcomer, and followed the salutation with a string of gibberish.
>
> Bulnes shook his head and replied in the modern Greek *dimotiki:* "Thanks, but who are you? Where are we?"
>
> More unintelligible sounds.
>
> "Is this," (Bulnes waved an arm) "Piriefs?"
>
> Light dawned on the stranger's face. *"Esti ho Peiraieus!"* he said, giving the name of the port its full Classical form, and then went off into another spate of chatter.[10]

Since Bulnes does not know Classical Greek, any words spoken in that language are to him mere sounds. The English cannot be given because that means going outside of Bulnes's mind. The full text of the remarks in Greek would be a mere jumble of noise to Bulnes. Besides, the reader will resent any long passages in a language that he does not understand. He will feel that the writer is showing off at his expense.

Later in the story, Bulnes learns Classical Greek. Thereafter, remarks "really" in Greek are all translated. At first Bulnes speaks Greek badly, which fact is indicated by broken English: "No; it are that we am going at Athens." Gradually he improves. To distinguish English that is supposedly Greek from the real English used by Bulnes and Flin when talking among themselves, the writer used a formalized English without contractions, among which were scattered a few Greek expressions translated literally: "Rejoice, O Sokrates!" or "By the Dog of Egypt!"

Do not use foreign words in place of English nouns outside of dialogue (as by calling French-fried potatoes *pommes frites*) unless there is no good English word for the object. In that case, the foreign word should be defined when introduced. Nor is it good to use a lot of foreign speech and then translate it all, thus:

> *"Mon dieu!* [My God!]" cried the *capitaine de corvette* [lieutenant-commander] commanding the *contretorpeilleur* [destroyer]. *"Nous sommes foutus!* [We're sunk!]"

☆ ☆ ☆

What if your characters are "really" speaking a past or future variety of English? If they are using past English, have them speak as the past speakers would have spoken unless the form is so archaic that it makes hard reading. You can use the English of the time of Johnson or Milton or Shakespeare and be understood. If, however, you go back to the time of Chaucer or earlier, you had better translate the language into modern English, perhaps retaining a few archaisms for flavor, but not so many as to impede the non-scholarly reader.

We may presume that English will go on changing (perhaps more slowly than hitherto because of the spread of literacy and world-wide intercommunication) so that in a thousand years it would be unintelligible. We must represent the speech of such a time in understandable English, but we may indicate futurity by a few made-up words or expressions. We can have fun by manufacturing the slang and obscenity of the future, as the words, however shocking to the futurians, would sound harmless to us.

Writers who served in one of the recent wars found that soldiers, like people of some other rough occupations, infuse their speech with a vast deal of profanity and obscenity. Such writers have sometimes thought that to be "realistic" and express their distaste for militarism, they had to use an equal amount of obscenity in their dialogue. But dialogue, as you know, is not a stenographic report of real speech. If you use a few four-letter words per story, you may get a strong effect, but if you use them on every page you get no effect at all.

☆ ☆ ☆

A writer can control the pace of any part of his story by letting the text contain more or less "dead matter" (description or exposition) and by narrating either fast physical action or slow. Suspense is effected by strong emotions on the part of the characters, by threats to their well-being, by bits of atmospheric description slyly dropped into the action, and by foreshadowing later incidents by hints or casual allusions, without either giving the show away or straining for effect with a sentence of the "had I but known" type.

As an example of foreshadowing, when Bulnes and Flin first visit the Acropolis, Flin exclaims:

"...Isn't it the most dashed wonderful thing you ever saw, Knut? Come on, there's the Parthenon!"

And off he galloped, sandals flapping. "No, the entrance is around the far end."

"Why," asked Bulnes, "should they put the entrance at the east end when you come up on to the Acropolis from the west? Does that make sense?"

"Some religious reason, or perhaps they wanted the rising sun to light the statue inside for dawn ceremonies. Isn't it beautiful?"

The Parthenon and the direction it faced were not mentioned to show off the author's research. Later in the story, Bulnes escapes from the Parthenon, so that its presence and orientation are essential plot elements. By introducing them in advance, the incidents of Bulnes's escape seem inevitable; whereas, had they been brought in at the time of the escape, the result would have appeared contrived.

Do not, however, give the reader a false lead—make a pother about something early in the story as if it were to be important when it really is not. Do not bring in something that looks like an important story element and then forget it, as Burroughs did with the hiss in Carter's cave.

Keep careful control of time. The story starts at a definite time, and everything happens at a definite time. These times are indicated to the reader, not necessarily by having the hero look at his watch, but by such means as mentioning sunrises and sunsets. Make sure that the times are those that would actually be required. If the hero is going anywhere, whether down the street or to Alpha Centauri, make sure that the time he takes is the correct one, whether he goes by foot or horseback or space ship. Use maps and timetables if need be. If you invent an imaginary city or country, draw a rough map of it. If the hero stabs the villain to death, unties the heroine, picks the lock on the door, dons his space suit, and leaps out into space, go through the motions of stabbing, untying and so on to see just how many seconds all those acts would actually take.

When the villain has the drop on the hero, do not assume that the hero can leap across the room and disarm the villain before he can pull his blaster trigger. It can't be done.

You need not narrate everything that happens between scenes. If nothing important has changed between them, simply indicate a space between lines for a lapse of time and plunge into the next scene. The reader will make the transition in his mind. If much time has passed, though, indicate the time of the new scene, as by mentioning that the hero has just finished lunch.

☆ ☆ ☆

Perhaps you are worrying about style. Style is essentially the way you write when you narrate imaginary events in the clearest, most concise and expressive manner you can. You do not achieve good style by deliberately imitating some older writer. What you achieve in such a case is a parody. Consider Hemingway's short, simple declarative sentences. While such sentences are useful, especially in describing fast physical action, longer and more complex sentences are more effective (and more economical of words) in reflective or explanatory sections. A narrative composed entirely of sentences of three and four words gives an unpleasantly jerky effect. Sentences, on the other hand, should never ramble down half a page or more. If they are that long, cut them up into shorter ones.

Avoid pleonasms and clichés. A pleonasm is an expression with superfluous words—a redundancy like "rich millionaire" or "old antique." (What other kinds of millionaires or antiques are there?) Other examples are "any sort *or kind*"; " 'You swine!' he said *insultingly*"; "weather *conditions*"; "*continue to* remain"; "I saw it *with my own eyes*"; "while *at the same time*"; "*mental* telepathy." All those italicized words are superfluous; weather, for example, *is* a condition.

A cliché is a worn-out phrase or figure of speech: "dazzling smile," "pearly teeth," "gleaming eyes," "lissom body," "lambent flame," and so on. The term is also applied to worn-out fictional elements or tricks, such as having the villain catch the hero, who escapes and catches the villain, who escapes and catches the hero, who...

Avoid also the stilted language that is common in government correspondence and corporation reports. This is the "officialese" that renders "Thank you" as "Appreciation is hereby expressed by the undersigned." It cultivates the passive voice, the obsequious omission of the pronoun "I," pseudo-learned Latinisms, and uncalled-for euphemisms and circumlocutions. It never uses one syllable where six will serve. If you mean "Smith was rich but Jones was poor," say so. Do not say, "It would appear that Smith belonged in one of the upper income brackets, while Jones was somewhat economically underprivileged."

The professional writer needs a large vocabulary, but he ought not to display it at every opportunity. In writing for juvenile readers, restrict your vocabulary to short, more common words, although not to the point of infantilism. In normal adult writing, if you have a choice between a shorter word and a longer, or a common word and a rare one, use the former except where you have good reason to use the latter—for euphony, say, or for variety. If "crab" turns up three or four times in two sentences, you are justified in changing one crab to a crustacean. Do not fear to use an uncommon word if it is the only one that exactly expresses your meaning, but do not use it merely to dazzle the reader. Clark Ashton Smith, in "The Testament of Athammaus," gained nothing by speaking of a "fulvous hide" when "tawny hide" would have done just as well.

Avoid unnecessary use of exclamation points and italics for emphasis. If you use exclamation points only rarely, say two or three times in a short story, they will be more effective when they do appear. There are exclamatory phrases like "How true!" or "What a surprise!" or "God forbid!" where the exclamation point is obligatory. But for most exclamatory sentences, the speaker's strong feeling is clear enough from his wording. Italics should be limited to such uses as foreign words and the names of ships, books, plays, poems, and periodicals, unless extraordinary emphasis is required, as in: "She looked out and shrieked: *The sun is blowing up!*"

An effective way to improve your style is to read your work aloud. By this means, you will discover many awkward sentences and other infelicities. You may find, for instance, that you have a habit of using the word "suddenly" several times on each page. In time you may learn by reading aloud to exploit the sound of words as well as their sense—to use occasional alliteration, or to write rhythmically, alternating stressed and unstressed syllables and using not more than two of the latter together.

The sense of what you wish to say, however, is the important thing. Say just what you want to say, with not an extra word, in such a manner that the reader will understand you perfectly the first time through, and style will take care of itself. It will appear like any other facet of your personality.

There are limits to the extent to which you can control your style. Certain things you do naturally and easily, and others you do with difficulty or not at all. Once we wrote an introduction for a book by a colleague, pointing out his peculiar characteristics and virtues (one doesn't stress faults in such a case). When our friend saw the piece, he wrote: "So that's what I do, is it? Between ourselves, I probably write that way because it's the only way I know how to write. Once or twice I've tried to change my style, but it always comes out the same."

SELLING

AN IMAGINATIVE STORY

obert Heinlein once advised the would-be writer to acquire these business habits: 1. write regularly; 2. finish what you start; 3. refrain from rewriting except to editorial order; 4. market the work promptly; and 5. push the work until it has been sold.[1] Heinlein admits that such rules are easier to expound than to apply. That, he said, is why he had no fear of giving away priceless trade secrets.

Heinlein's third maxim is arguable. The number of drafts that you make depends on several factors. One is the way an individual works. With some people, the unconscious acts like a well-adjusted concrete mixer, which turns out a smooth mix that can be used immediately. With others, the material that issues forth is uneven in quality and requires additional attention.

If you can type the first draft of a story with all the polish of a finished piece, you are unusually skilled or gifted. To develop ideas, to correct punctuation, and to polish style, two or even three revisions are usually required. It is hard, for example, to do sure, powerful characterizations the first time through the typewriter. It is equally difficult to tie up all loose ends.

Heinlein is right in saying that you must not simply rewrite and rewrite in search of perfection. Rewriting diminishes your effective word rate because you have produced more words for the amount of money you can expect to get. Still, the creative artist in any serious writer overrides the materialist and goads the writer into doing his very best. He knows his readers will be disappointed if the story does not live up to its possibilities, and the loyal readers are the people who enable any author to ply his trade. He knows, also, that even a great idea inadequately handled is less salable than one with a mediocre idea stunningly set forth.

☆ ☆ ☆

When, at last, you write your final draft, type with a black ribbon, reasonably fresh, on white typewriter paper of average grade. Either make two carbon copies, or—if you can afford it—one carbon for your files and one Xerox of the ribbon copy. The latter is ideal for further reproduction; but a typed copy made with fresh carbon paper will serve and saves the writer money.

Type with double spacing, on one side of the paper only. Leave margins of about an inch at top, bottom, and along both sides of the page. If your typewriter lacks an attachment for indicating when you are nearing the bottom of the page, you can easily mark a number of pages in advance with a warning mark. To do this, riffle a goodly number of sheets with your fingers until they overlap slightly, then draw a line across the row of edges with a soft pencil about an inch from the bottom. Each page will then have a tick of black to remind you to insert a new sheet as necessary.

The first page should carry the title of the story and the name and address of the author. Typing a separate title sheet is optional; such a page is more appropriate for a novel than for a short story. Number each page at the center of the top line.

Start each chapter on a fresh page. To show a gap between lines (as at the end of a scene or section) three asterisks or the symbol # may be typed in the middle of the blank line. If your break comes at the end of a page of manuscript, indicate it anyway, to signal the printer that you wish a blank space to appear at that place when the manuscript is set in print.

Indicate a dash by a pair of hyphens separated by a space from adjacent words—not by a single hyphen or by a hyphen adjacent to the preceding or following word. If your typewriter has no *1* key, use a lower-case *l* for the numeral one, not a capital *I*. Indicate the end of a story by a row of #-signs, or by the words "The End." Otherwise, if the story ends near the bottom of a page, the editor may worry lest he has lost some of your manuscript.

Follow the rules that you learned in school about indenting, paragraphing, punctuating, and the like. If you are uncertain about English usage, get an up-to-date English grammar. If you are writing for a big book-publishing company, ask them to send you a copy of their style manual and follow it. Some companies have a definite policy about punctuating sentences and hyphenating words that may commonly appear in more than one form. Once you decide which form to use, be consistent throughout the work.

The manuscript should be reasonably clean—not perfect, as if for a thesis, but easy to read. Four or five minor corrections on a page are not objectionable; fifteen or twenty corrections, or interpolations written up and down the margins, call for retyping. Do not try to erase and retype every mistake, especially if you are typing in triplicate. If you discover the typo at the time you make it, *x* out the word and retype it. If you are typing a single copy with the intention of photocopying it, use a chalk-covered tape or white correction fluid, which can be bought at the stationer's, to blank out a mistyped symbol or word, and then type the correct symbol over it. If you discover the error when you are reading the finished manuscript, make the correction with a pen or pencil. The editor will not mind, and you will save precious seconds.

Learn the standard proof-reader's marks and use them. You will find them in *Webster's New International Dictionary* and in the leaflets that some publishers issue as guides for their copy editors and authors. For instance, if you inadvertently capitalize a word, type the virgule (/) through it, thus: "Come Ⱨere." This is the printer's symbol for changing a capital letter to lower-case. Corrections made on one copy should be made on all. If several lines in a paragraph are badly fouled by corrections, one can retype that paragraph, glue it over the old one, and get a photocopy of the improved page. The Xerox machine has greatly simplified the problems of making corrections and extra copies of manuscripts.

How many copies of each work should you have? Never type the final draft of *anything*—a story, an article, or even a business letter—without making at least one carbon copy. Of every major piece of literary work, the author needs two copies in addition to the ribbon copy. Some editors demand two copies. One copy, at least, must be kept in the author's file at all times.

Editors refuse to accept responsibility for lost manuscripts. Yet, manuscripts do get lost, either in the mail or on the high-piled desks of editors. Even sending manuscripts by insured parcel post or registered mail cannot guarantee their safe arrival. Certainly, no amount of money paid by the Postal Service a year later will make up for the time wasted and the anguish suffered by an author whose only copy has been lost or destroyed. A stamped, self-addressed post card clipped to the first page of a manuscript, stating that the editor at *Analog* has received your story, is a clever device for letting the writer know that the editor has the manuscript. Even the busiest editor will drop such a card into the mailbox.

When a story appears in a magazine, get two or three extra file copies, in case you are ever reduced to your last carbon copy just when somebody wants the text for anthology, movie, or other subsidiary use. Manuscripts bought by magazine publishers are not normally returned, although those bought by book publishers are usually returned upon request. The writer is well-advised to ask for the return of all book manuscripts. They will become valuable as well as useful when you become famous or even reasonably successful.

☆ ☆ ☆

It is hard for a writer to know whether his writing is good, or whether he is on the wrong track. A writer's own opinion of his product has little relationship to the reaction of editors or readers. Often a piece that a writer dislikes is enthusiastically received by others, while the story he thinks his best may be judged harshly.

A beginner, therefore, may wish someone to read and criticize his manuscripts. A writer thinks first of those nearest to him; family, spouse, or friends. But the average partner or pal is not competent to give fair and informed criticism. Even if somebody is willing to read your material and knows enough about fiction to criticize it perceptively, it is difficult to persuade him to say what he thinks without fear or favor.

We all like to be told that we are good, and there is no mistaking the dismay on the face of a writer who has just heard that his brain child is a deformed idiot. For this reason, your nearest and dearest are particularly unreliable critics. They love you (or at least have to live with you); and they are, therefore, reluctant to say anything that will hurt you or make you harder to get along with. No matter how awful the opus, they are likely to wrap their criticism in such gentle euphemisms and qualifications that you may never realize that they do not like the piece at all.

If you find a willing and competent critic, do not spoil him as a source of criticism by reacting badly to his remarks. Do not rage, lament, sulk, or argue. If you embarrass or antagonize your critic, he will avoid such treatment in the future by refusing to read your efforts or by giving you encouraging blather in place of helpful advice.

Writers' conferences as a source of professional criticism have been dealt with already. Some literary agents will read and criticize manuscripts for a fee. In writers' magazines, one sees advertisements by people who offer to read and criticize manuscripts for a stated amount of money. Professional writers sometimes will undertake to criticize another writer's manuscript, but they, too, demand payment.

Such a demand is legitimate. To read and report on a short story takes at least an hour or two. To perform the same service for a novel is a good day's work or more. There is no reason why you should expect such service free from anyone not bound to you by ties of blood or friendship, any more than you should walk into a physician's office and ask him to spend a few hours explaining some point of medical science. Although there is no standard rate for reading services, a writer should expect to pay $20 to $25 for a short story, and up to $100 for a novel. Beware of charges much higher or much lower than these figures. An advertiser who charges twice these rates might be overestimating the worth of his services, while one who agrees to read a manuscript for a dollar or two could not possibly give each piece proper attention and still make a living.

There is a great deal of racketeering in the field of manuscript criticism. It usually takes the form of giving each piece only cursory attention—glancing over a few pages—and writing the author a few canned paragraphs of generalities and clichés: "The story is colorful, but the plot wants further tightening up. . . The heroine's character needs to be more thoroughly developed. . ." and so on.

Such critics, moreover, never discourage the writer of even the most hopeless tripe. Thousands of people would like to write fiction professionally but cannot. It would be kinder to inform them early in the game how far below professional standards their work appears to be, so that they either learn to write a great deal better or decide to write for pleasure only, without spending time and expense on a hopeless task.

Few individuals or institutional critics care to be so brutally frank. Even when you receive what appears to be an honest criticism from an editor or a paid critic, you must downgrade his comments because of the universal tendency to say nice things to soften bad news. If your critic says: "This is splendid. I enjoyed it immensely," the piece may be just barely salable. If he says: "Although this story has many virtues, it is not quite suitable for publication in its present form," the chance is that the story is a stinker.

In recent years, a number of courses—seminars, rather—have been offered in creative writing, by various universities. In the best of these, attendees are expected to bring a few of their own manuscripts for criticism and rewriting; and they are encouraged to write more stories during the seminar. Established science-fiction writers are often visiting instructors at these seminars. Although we have had no direct experience with these affairs, they are well spoken of by some of our colleagues; and several new writers credit their successful start to them.

☆ ☆ ☆

Many new writers wonder about enlisting the help of a literary agent. Agents who sell in the American or domestic market charge 10% of gross earnings as a commission; those who sell the work of an American writer in a foreign country charge 20%. Fine, you may say; I'll be glad to pay for their know-how.

But it is not so easy as that. First of all, literary agents rarely accept as a client any writer until he has sold several pieces to reputable magazines or book publishers. Thus, just when you are most in need of help, few agents, if any, will bother with you. Then, when you become a "promising author" and have learned a thing or two about marketing a literary creation, you will find that it is hard to locate an agent who will give you and your works the undivided attention you feel you deserve. Like a marriage, this is a personal relationship that must be built up bit by bit.

Some writers do find agents who are supportive, who act as editors of their works, who lend them money in lean times, and so on. But many agents are busy and hasty. They often accept whatever contract the publisher sees fit to offer their clients, not noticing, or bothering to fight for, such elementary clauses as those covering termination and bankruptcy. We have learned by painful experience never to accept with blind faith a contract negotiated by an agent. After all, when *your* work and *your* livelihood are at stake, you must rely upon your own knowledge and care to make sure the contract is favorable and clearly worded.

A writer must always remember that an agent wears more than one hat: he is not only your agent, but also the agent for dozens of other writers. Moreover, he must remain on good terms with the various editors with whom he deals. Since he goes to lunch with them, sends them only the material they are likely to want, and derives a living from the advance royalties they pay out, he would rather keep on their good side than pander to any particular writer whose book or two he undertakes to sell.

Agents, moreover, seldom even try to sell to the science-fiction magazines. Certainly, there are not enough commissions to be had from a short story or article selling at three cents a word to interest an agent in the clerical work of reading, listing, mailing, storing, and eventually returning magazine pieces to undistinguished writers. Since our readers are likely to start their writing careers with sales to science-fiction or fantasy magazines, they must learn how to market their own works; to keep their own records of submissions, returns and resubmissions; to study, bargain, and eventually file contracts; to preserve letters to and from the buyers; to note when payments are due and when they are made; and to record, for tax deductions, the expenses of writing supplies, postage, and office maintenance. Writers who have no head for business may not even have a garret roof over their heads for long.

Still, for writers who do not live in or near New York and thus cannot visit editors personally, for writers who do not specialize in one type of writing so that they can keep track of the market themselves, for writers who have no knowledge of the commercial side of writing, an agent can be helpful indeed. If you shop among fellow writers for an agent who might take you on, you will come upon the curious fact that no two clients will give you a consistent picture of a given agent. One author may say: "He's wonderful! He really made a writer out of me." Another author, asked about the same man, will howl: "I wouldn't trust that crook again if. . . ." You can never be sure how you will get along with an agent until you try one. But if you dislike one or feel his services are shoddy, you are not obligated to stay with him for other than the piece of writing he has already sold for you. Never sign an agency agreement that ties you to the agent for future works.

Some agents are unethical or incompetent—not many but enough to be worth watching for. One fellow made a practice of selling foreign rights and pocketing the money. When caught red-handed by the Authors Guild, he said: "Well, you don't expect me to live in a penthouse and drive a Mercedes on 10%, do you?"

Agents have been known to claim to represent authors

with whom they had no agreements; to lure away the clients of other agents; to represent publishers as well as authors and thus to collect double commissions; to try to collect a commission to which they were not entitled, as on a sale made after the author had severed connections with them; to sell the same story to two anthologists without warning either; to use their clients' money for their own expenses; and to forbid clients to correspond directly with their editors. Some agents merely act as mailing centers, sending out everything they are given without helping their authors to improve marginal stories, or fitting the stories to the needs of the publisher, or demanding the best possible rates and terms for their clients.

Do not let this catalogue of malefaction discourage you if you really need an agent. After all, a similar indictment could be drawn up against individual lawyers or physicians. Most agents are as honest as other people, and a good agent can often make more money for you than you can make for yourself.

There are several ways of selecting an agent. You can ask the advice of colleagues, although such advice must be taken with reservations. You can write to the Society of Authors' Representatives, currently at 101 Park Avenue, New York, 10003. The society maintains a professional standard of ethics among its members, requiring them to refrain from advertising, to keep their clients' money in bank accounts separate from their own, and to pay their clients within a fixed time after they receive the money from publishers. The society will send you a copy of its rules and a list of its members.

There are half a dozen agents considered more or less specialists in the field of imaginative fiction. You can identify them by writing to the editors of the major science-fiction magazines. Among the larger non-specialist agencies, there is sometimes one member of the firm who specializes in imaginative fiction. Such, for example, is the case with the Scott Meredith Agency, one of the largest in the country, with branch offices in several foreign capitals.

☆ ☆ ☆

When an agent accepts a client, the client does not ordinarily sign a formal contract. He simply sends the agent his material. The agent sells it if he can, receives payment from the publisher, and sends the client a check for ninety percent of the amount received, retaining ten percent as his commission. This rate applies to all transactions involving literary property, with the exceptions of motion-picture and foreign sales, where two agents and two commissions may be necessary. While you might not agree formally to give an agent the exclusive right to handle all your work, you operate on the tacit agreement to do so, unless he understands otherwise. Vagueness in such matters is one of the best ways to bring about agent trouble. You should not let an agent think that he is handling all your material, and then sell a juicy piece behind his back. Nor should you send a story to two or three of the best-paying markets and then, when they have rejected it, expect the agent to send it to the low-paying publishers. If he is to share in your defeats, he is entitled to share in your triumphs.

Because agent-client relationships are commonly made by word-of-mouth agreements, the rights of both persons form a legal grey area that can prove very difficult when disagreements arise. A few of the largest literary agencies have a printed agency agreement for the author to sign. If the agent you choose does not have such an agreement, you might type up a letter, similar to the example that follows, with one copy for your files and one for the agent, each copy to be signed by both of you.

September 31, 1975

MacSmith Literary Agency
4995 13th Avenue
New York NY 10101

Dear Mr. MacSmith:

I am writing this letter of agreement to set forth our author-agent relationship. If you agree to the terms, will you kindly so indicate by signing one copy and returning it to me.

I, as author, give you, as literary agent, the

exclusive right, for the duration of this agreement, to offer for sale all my literary works, to make contracts for the sale of these works, subject to my approval, and to receive the payments and royalties from such sales as long as the original contracts with the publisher shall remain in force, provided that you carry out the terms of this agreement.

All monies received or collected by you for my account shall be placed in a bank account, in escrow, and kept separate from your personal funds. From monies received on royalties earned in the United States, its territories, and Canada, you shall deduct, as your commission, 10%; except that in the case of motion picture, television, or radio use of my works, you shall deduct 15%. From monies received which were earned in countries other than the United States, its territories, and Canada, you shall deduct 20%, this percentage to include commissions paid to or deducted by foreign agents through whom such sales were negotiated.

You agree that, within ten days of receipt of any monies, you will render an accounting of amounts received and send me 90% of receipts of any and all domestic sales (those made in the United States, its territories and Canada), 85% of monies received from motion picture, television, or radio sales, and 80% of receipts from foreign sales, together with the buyer's or publisher's statement showing the period covered, the gross amount received, the number of dollars deducted, and the net amount sent to me.

A year-end statement, listing all monies received and all agency fees paid therefrom, shall be rendered during the month of January each year for aid in preparation of my income tax.

You further agree to use your best efforts to promote the sale of my works as expeditiously as possible, giving due regard to their submission to the best-paying markets in the first instance, and to obtaining the best terms in every sale. You will see that every contract with a publisher contains a clause covering termination of the contract and a clause providing for automatic termination in case of bankruptcy, said clause to read as follows:

"If (a) a petition in bankruptcy is filed by the publisher, or (b) a petition in bankruptcy is filed against the publisher and such petition is finally sustained, or (c) a petition for an arrangement under Title XI of the Federal Bankruptcy Act is filed by the publisher or a petition for reorganization is filed by or against the publisher or a meeting is called of the publisher's creditors, or (d) the publisher makes an assignment for the benefit of creditors, or (e) the publisher liquidates its business for any cause whatsoever, the author may terminate this agreement by written notice and thereupon all rights granted hereunder shall revert to the author."

In the event that you fail to render accounts and pay the monies entrusted to you by the publisher within the given time, I may, at my option, terminate this agreement by sending you a certified or registered letter, with return receipt requested, so stating.

This agreement may, at the option of either party, be terminated by means of a certified or registered letter sent to the other party to this agreement, with a return receipt requested. Provided that you have complied with the terms of this agreement, works already negotiated by you for my benefit under this authority shall continue to be managed by you. You shall have the sole right to make subsidiary sales, foreign sales, or other sales of such rights as are excluded from the original publisher's contracts, so long as these publishing contracts made by you remain in force.

Should any dispute arise that cannot be settled amicably between us, the matter shall be settled by arbitration according to the laws of the State of New York; and the decision of the arbitrators shall be binding upon both parties.

If you approve of the foregoing terms, please sign two copies of this agreement, keep one copy for your files, and return the other copy to me.

Sincerely yours,

_____

Karen O'Jones

Approved and accepted:

_____

Henry MacSmith

Dated: _____

Although such an agreement protects both parties, a writer must make certain that the agreement he signs contains no clause that binds him to the agent for works yet unwritten. Only those stories that the agent undertakes to sell and sells should come under the agency agreement. Additional money from works once sold by an agent continues to be properly collected by that agent. New works, however, are the author's sole property until he puts them into the hands of the agent.

☆ ☆ ☆

Let us suppose that you decide to sell your stories directly, without an agent. First, be sure that you are sending the right kind of manuscript in the right kind of envelope, carton, or other container.

Do not send manuscripts rolled, or sewn together, or bound up in a fancy folder. The manuscript may be sent flat or folded, depending upon how thick it is. If you send it flat, put a cardboard stiffener in the envelope. A thin manuscript can be folded twice and inserted in an ordinary legal-sized letter envelope. A thicker one can be folded once and placed in a 6" x 9" manila clasp envelope. A still thicker manuscript should be sent flat in a 9" x 12" or 10" x 13" envelope.

For manuscripts of book-length novels, use boxes, especially typewriter-paper boxes, which you save for the purpose. Wrap such parcels well with strong paper and lots of string. A manuscript that has been through the Christmas postal rush can be a pretty pathetic object. If, after repeated mailings, the first or the last page gets badly battered, retype it. Small manuscripts (short stories and novelettes) usually go by first-class mail, but the manuscript of a novel can be mailed much more cheaply if the package is marked "Manuscript: Special Fourth-Class Rate. Letter Enclosed."

The manuscript should be accompanied by a covering letter, or at least a short note, formally addressed and stating that you are submitting for consideration such-and-such a story, so many words long. (Estimate your wordage by counting several pages chosen at random, computing your average words per page, and multiplying by the number of pages, with allowance for partly blank pages.) Do not plead with the editor or tell him how fervently you hope that he will like the story. He will decide that for himself when he reads it.

Editors expect authors to send return postage with their manuscripts. If you do not send return postage, and the editor rejects your story, he will probably send you a post card demanding this postage before he will return your manuscript. If, however, you are a regular contributor to his magazine, he may overlook this formality in the case of small manuscripts.

While the editor has the manuscript, do not harass him, asking whether he is going to take the story—at least not until he has had it for four to five weeks. The manuscript is buried somewhere in a large pile of manuscripts. He will come to it in due course and make known his pleasure. You should not, unless you know him pretty well and have some special reason for asking a favor, ask him to consider your manuscript out of turn.

If the manuscript is useless, as are most of those he gets, he will send it back with a printed rejection slip. Some publishers have a convenient kind of slip on which they can check off one of a number of reasons for rejection. While a rejection slip is no insult—we all get them—if the story is almost good enough to take, the editor may instead write you a letter.

We asked several editors of imaginative-fiction magazines for their most common reasons for rejecting stories. The two reasons mentioned most often were, first, triteness or lack of originality; and second, lack of characterization.

Lack of originality means that the writer has nothing in particular to say. He is merely imitating older stories, or has based his story upon an idea which, though perhaps new to him, is old and worn-out among the aficionados. This fault is common in stories submitted by general, or mainstream, writers who think that they would like to try the imaginative field without knowing much about it.

Lack of characterization means that the writer is using stock, cardboard stereotypes for characters, or that his people lack any characterization at all. For instance, they may all talk alike, the way the writer himself does; or the story may have no comprehensible human values and motivations.

Mentioned almost as frequently as these two causes of rejection was poor writing. The English is defective, or the sentences are awkward, or the dialogue is absurd. Perhaps the story is badly developed, or there is no climax, or the writer does not know other aspects of fictional craftsmanship.

Less often mentioned was the fault variously called slowness, dullness, or lack of entertainment value. Such a fault may arise from having too much idea and not enough story. More rarely, editors mentioned the opposite fault: too much story and too few ideas. An example of this is the typical space opera, an adventure story with a few gadgets thrown in to make it technically science fiction. Editors vary in this regard. One likes a story that another considers too gadgety or intellectual, while the second likes a story that the first deemed a mere rodeo with rocketry.

Minor causes of rejection were the use of inconclusive endings—unstructured stories that merely state a situation without resolving it; sloppy or illegible manuscripts; stories submitted to the wrong market, such as a fantasy submitted to a magazine that takes only straight science fiction; or straight adventure stories submitted to an imaginative-fiction magazine. Sometimes a magazine gets so overstocked, or the editor's pile of unread manuscripts gets so out of hand, that he has to send stories back unread for want of time.

Sometimes an editor will reject a story that has nothing

definitely wrong with it—but nothing definitely right with it either. It is not a bad story, but not compelling, and the editor will be driven to curious shifts to find a definite reason for rejection. Such a story can sometimes be made salable by a rewrite, incorporating new and interesting ideas.

All these faults and virtues are relative. No story is perfect. If they were all up to the highest standard, the editors would still have to reject most of them for lack of space. On the other hand, the editors have to buy many stories embodying the faults listed above for want of anything better. Judging from the number of bad stories printed, there is plenty of room in the field for good stories. We doubt whether any first-class story today, whose author vigorously presses its sale, fails to find a market. The difficult task is to write that really good story.

If an editor rejects a story, do not argue with him, or write him angry letters, or indulge in other displays of temperament. The professional writer has to learn to turn a stony face to disappointment. If you annoy an editor who is merely trying to perform his job, you lessen your chance of future sales to him.

Never try to save postage by asking one editor, if he rejects a story, to send it directly to another editor. While every editor knows that many of the stories he buys have been rejected by others, it is tactless to remind him of the fact. And, try though he will to read each story with a mind unbiased by knowledge of the author's name or the manuscript's history, the editor can hardly help being influenced in a doubtful case by the certain knowledge that one of his colleagues has already judged the piece adversely.

In the early part of their careers, writers should not send photocopies of their works to a prospective buyer. Some editors refuse, out of hand, to look at anything but the ribbon copy of a story or novel, because they believe that a photocopy proves the writer is showing his work to several editors at once.

From the author's point of view, of course, sending copies to more than one editor at a time increases the chance of a quick sale. But only those who have reached the pinnacle of success can "hold an auction"—frankly offer the work to several publishers and notify them all that the work will be sold to the highest bidder. Most writers have to submit their works to one publisher at a time, wait an anxious six weeks, receive a rejection slip stoically, and ship the work out again and again.

☆ ☆ ☆

To locate the most likely publishers to show their stories to, authors are permitted—even encouraged—to write identical letters to two or three editors describing the piece and asking if they would like to look at it. Today, in fact, this preliminary step is almost essential to obtain a reading for your material. Many editors, awash in manuscripts, simply send back unread all unsolicited manuscripts. Only those sent by agents or those that they have agreed to look at are given a place on their crowded desks.

In choosing which editor to approach, consider his rates, his preferences, and his magazine's policies. Of these, the most important is rates. You should keep a list of all the likely outlets for your stories and the rates that each pays. If two editors offer the same rates but one allows the author to retain more of the subsidiary rights—such as foreign and motion picture rights—his contract would be the more desirable. He would be placed at the top of your list.

As you send the manuscript out, moving down your list towards the lower-paying markets, be sure to record the date of submission, the name and address of the editor, and on evidence of its arrival, the date it was received by the editor. A polite follow-up note in six weeks is permissible. This, too, should be noted on the list.

If a story unsuccessfully makes the rounds of every editor you thought worth contacting, do not throw it away. It might be a poor story but contain the germ of an idea that may later prove useful. The editors may be starting a new magazine in a couple of years and be desperate for even undistinguished stories. A paperback book publisher might someday be glad to put it into a collection of your early works. Or, it may be that the story is out of favor because it is currently out of style. For several years in the late 1960s,

New Wave (*avant-garde*, stream-of-consciousness) stories were popular. Good old rollicking science fiction was plain, old-fashioned, and undesired. In the mid-1970s, the pendulum of taste swung back. Now, old-style, well-structured science-fiction stories are called "classic" and are much in demand.

Some of our readers may ask: how does one get a story into an anthology? Normally, the man or woman who edits the anthology makes all his own choices. If he wants one of your tales, he will get in touch with you, through your publisher if he does not know how else to reach you. Anthologists do not ordinarily pay a great deal of money—one to two hundred dollars is all one can expect for the pre-published story. However, the anthologist is buying only one-time use of the material on a *non-exclusive* basis. If he wants all rights, do not sell him the story. Non-exclusive use means that the author still retains the right to resell the material to anyone at any time. Although it might be unwise to sell the story to two anthologists whose work is expected out next year, you must keep the right to do so, and that word "non-exclusive" is the word you need to protect the right to do so.

From time to time, review the contracts for the stories you have sold. You may find that you have valuable rights—foreign, anthology, motion-picture, paperback reprint, or whatever—that you can exploit. Often these bring in much more money than the original sale. Never, never, sell "all rights" to anything. Good publishers do not demand it; shoddy publishers will prey on a young writer if he isn't aware of his markets and the custom of the trade. There will be more on this subject in the following chapter.

☆ ☆ ☆

Some writers give much thought to the matter of a pseudonym. Pseudonyms may be adopted for a variety of reasons. If your name is John J. Smith or Anaxagoras X. Szczebrzeszinski, anyone could understand your wish to change it. Some writers adopt pseudonyms because their families do not approve of their profession or because their employers would be displeased that they are writing "that stuff." An employer's objections changed Harry Clement Stubbs into Hal Clement.

Occasionally, a writer finds that his real name is associated with writing of a particular kind and decides to use another name for his imaginative tales. Sometimes an editor wishes to run two pieces by one author in one issue of his magazine; but because of a common tabu against having two appearances of one name on the contents page, he will ask the author to submit a pseudonym for one of the stories. Some writers adopt pen names for no reason except the urge to make-believe.

Unless there is some compelling reason to do otherwise, it is best to use your own name on all your work, unless the editor insists on a house name. If you write in a variety of styles, you will benefit for the reputation for versatility and volume.

It is, moreover, important to get your name before your public and to keep it there as much as possible. In today's professional world, self-promotion is a must. There is no better way to make your name a household word than to write as many good stories as you can and do newsworthy things so that your name will appear in print or on the air. National television shows, such as *Today*, and *Bookbeat*, give so much coverage that a book discussed thereon is likely to sell a whole printing as a result of the exposure. It must never be forgotten, however, that publicity is fine only so long as it does not interfere with a writer's *metier*.

THE BUSINESS SIDE OF WRITING

A writer's first published work carries him beyond the reach of reason. In fact, a little star dust accompanies each letter of acceptance as long as a writer lives. Still, unless writing is to remain an avocation while some pedestrian job pays the monthly bills, it is just as important to learn the business side of writing as it is to master the skills of plotting, characterization, and finding a buyer for one's story.

Negotiating a contract for a literary work requires considerable knowledge of contract law and psychology. If you show yourself unduly eager to sell the piece, you will receive the minimum price. On the other hand, if you hold your work in such exaggerated regard that you refuse the going rate, you may lose a worthwhile sale.

To avoid both pitfalls, a writer must learn what clauses a trade-book contract contains, what terms to insist on, and what terms might or might not be negotiable for a person in his position. Since publishers are thoroughly familiar with their contracts and the custom of the trade, and since most authors are not, an inexperienced writer, acting alone, is at a disadvantage in negotiating a contract. Fortunately, it is not necessary to act alone. The Authors Guild, of 234 West 44th Street, New York, New York 10036, is an organization of approximately 4,000 writers, who have banded together to improve the lot of all authors in such matters as copyright protection, taxation, legislation, and freedom of expression.

[173]

In 1972, the Authors Guild published a Model Trade Book Contract, which caused a stir throughout the publishing industry. The seven-page form with its accompanying interpretive Contract Guide is available to all members of the Authors Guild and is, by itself, worth far more than the price of an annual membership in the Guild. In fact, next to a typewriter, the Model Contract is the single most valuable tool available to any writer, new or experienced.

By studying the Guide and comparing the various terms of the Model Contract with the terms of the contract offered by a publisher, even a tyro can soon find out what clauses are essential for the protection of his literary property. Had such an aid been available years ago when the de Camps sold all rights to several novels to a small publisher for the magnificent sum of $300 per book, they would not have to share with that publisher the thousands of dollars that those same works now earn from paperback and foreign sales.

Writers specializing in the field of imaginative fiction may also—although to a lesser degree—profit from membership in the Science Fiction Writers of America. This organization has various classes of membership; basically, it admits as full, active members only those writers who have already made a sale of science fiction or fantasy to a professional market, and have done so within the last year or so. The exact rules change from time to time; for details, consult the organization's executive secretary, who can be reached through any science-fiction magazine or book editor.

The SFWA holds meetings during the various fan conventions at which professional writers gather. It sponsors a dinner meeting each spring, at which Nebula Awards are made for outstanding work and the problems of writing and publishing science fiction are discussed. The SFWA has also issued for the use of its members a suggested trade book and a paperback book contract directed toward works in the field of imaginative fiction. Writers who prove eligible for membership in the SFWA will find these contracts helpful.

☆ ☆ ☆

What are the major clauses that an equitable trade book contract should contain? To do the subject justice, far more space would be required than is here available, but some of the main points can be discussed. While a new writer may not be able to demand all these provisions, he should at least know what terms are desirable and strive to gain as many of them as possible.

1. Rights should be licensed to the publisher for the original term of copyright (28 years), not for the original and the renewal term (a total of 56 years).

2. Copyright should be taken out in the name of the author; and, if the publisher is granted the right to make foreign sales, he should be responsible for making certain that the foreign publisher likewise secures proper copyright protection for the work. The author himself should secure the renewal copyright or make sure that his publisher does so.

3. If the author delivers a manuscript as specified in the contract, and the publisher decides that the manuscript is unsatisfactory after paying part or all of the advance, the author should be obliged to repay not more than 30% of the advance, and then only after he has resold the work to another publisher.

4. On adult hardcover books, royalty rates should be at least 10% of retail price for the first 5,000 copies; 12½% on the next 2,500 or 5,000; and 15% thereafter. Children's books usually command lower royalty rates but remain in print much longer. (Recognized authors now often get rates that start at 12½% and step up to 15% and even to 17½%. However, most publishers pay far lower royalty rates on Canadian, book club, and "special sales." It is wise to insist on a floor beneath which royalties on quantity discounts may not go: 66% of the regular rate is good, 50% acceptable. On paper-backed books, royalty rates should start not lower than 6% for the first 150,000 copies and increase to 8% or even 10% as the number of sales increases.)

5. Accounting periods should be clearly stated in the contract, and the date of statements and payments should not exceed two months thereafter.

6. If the publisher should sublicense a paperbacked edition of a trade book, he should be permitted to withhold only a limited amount, say 30% of the paperback publisher's advance, to cover any advances already paid the author.

7. Money from such paperback sales or from the sale of foreign or motion picture and television rights must be reported to the author promptly, and payment of proceeds must be made within 14 days of receipt and not held for months until the next half-yearly accounting period.

8. In case of a suit against the publisher for libel, copyright infringement, or invasion of privacy, the author's liability should be limited to final judgments. Moreover, the amount payable by the author should be limited to 30% or 50% of the total judgment. While the case is in progress, the author's royalties should not be entirely withheld.

9. In nearly every contract, termination is allowed when the book goes out of print. Unfortunately, all too seldom is the term "out of print" clearly defined. An author should insist that when sales drop below a stated number per year, the book shall be considered out of print. Then all rights must be returned to the writer upon written request sent by registered mail, unless the publisher agrees to republish and republishes the work within a period of 6 months. For a hardbacked edition where the royalty per copy is in the neighborhood of $1.00, a book might be termed out of print when annual sales are fewer than 100 copies and royalties for the year fall below $100. For a paperbacked novel, sales of less than 1,500 copies or an annual royalty of $100 might be defined as out of print.

10. Finally, no contract should be accepted unless it has a well-drawn bankruptcy clause. A poorly-drawn bankruptcy clause may permit a bankrupt publisher who undertakes a reorganization under Title XI of the Federal Bankruptcy Act to retain the rights to a book even though the book is unobtainable and no royalties are paid to the author. A fool-proof bankruptcy clause

would automatically return to the author all rights if the publisher goes into voluntary bankruptcy, involuntary bankruptcy, or reorganization under Title XI. Failure to include all three types of insolvency has caused many authors (including the de Camps) to lose a great deal of income and to become involved in lengthy and costly litigation. A sound bankruptcy clause, such as that already described in connection with an agent's agreement, should read thus:

> If (a) a petition in bankruptcy is filed by the Publisher, or (b) a petition in bankruptcy is filed against the Publisher and such petition is finally sustained, or (c) a petition for an arrangement under Title XI of the Federal Bankruptcy Act is filed by the Publisher, or a petition for reorganization is filed by or against the Publisher, or a meeting is called of the Publisher's creditors, or (d) the Publisher makes an assignment for the benefit of creditors, or (e) the Publisher liquidates its business for any cause whatsoever, the Author may terminate this Agreement by written notice and thereupon all rights granted by him hereunder shall revert immediately to him.

If the contract lacks such a clause, insist that it be inserted as a rider. Many contracts have several riders attached, covering provisions demanded by knowledgeable authors.

Several other contract terms give writers additional protection when they can persuade the publisher to accept them. Some of these are only now coming into general use. A few, at least, may be inserted as riders if you ask for them before signing your contract.

1. Demand that no advertising or additional material be inserted into the book without the author's permission.
2. Ask to be consulted about the dust jacket, and insist on writing the jacket flap material yourself. By so doing, you will give the reader a taste of your writing style and an accurate biographical sketch.

3. See that the contract accords the author the right to read the proofs to make sure that errors are corrected.
4. Permit no sale of overstock nor discount sales of the title for the first two years after publication.
5. Allow no cheap edition to be published before six months after the date of the original publication.
6. Delete the clause that gives the publisher an automatic privilege of publishing the author's next book. If an author feels loyal to his publisher, he will usually be glad to offer him the next book.
7. If the publisher fails to send prompt and regular semi-annual statements and payments, or to pay money due from advances on subsidiary sales, or to comply with all the other terms of the contract, the contract may be terminated by the author, merely by sending a registered letter to the publisher.
8. All rights not specifically granted under the contract shall be reserved to the author.
9. The publisher may not assign the contract without the written consent of the author.
10. Unearned royalties from other books should not be deducted from earnings on the current contract.

☆ ☆ ☆

The reader may wonder what kind of advance royalties a book-length work might command. Much depends, of course, on the originality of the tale, the quality of the writing, and the name and reputation of the author. If the work is a run-of-the-mill but competent novel in the field of imaginative fiction, a new writer might be offered $1,500 from a publisher like Doubleday with a 10% royalty rate to the first 5,000 copies. This means that, if the book were to sell at $6.95, the author would get 69½ cents on every copy sold at retail. Copies given to reviewers, damaged, or returned by booksellers, naturally, receive no royalty at all. So, 2,159 copies would have to sell before the advance royalty of $1,500 would be earned. Books sold at retail thereafter would continue to earn 69½ cents each. Such an undistinguished book might sell 3,000 copies, possibly 4,000, giving the writer a total return on his investment in time and brain power of $2,780 over a period of a year or two.

An experienced writer or someone with a stunningly original plot or a name like Verne Wells Asimov would, in today's market, command for a hardcover book an advance well in excess of $10,000 and perhaps royalties starting at 12½%, soon moving up to 15%. His book might sell 20,000 copies or even 30,000 and be selected for one of the many book clubs run by the larger publishing houses. If the writer had had the foresight to peddle the novel first to a magazine for something like $2,000, and if, eventually, the title were to be licensed to a mass-market paperback publisher, he might net in the neighborhood of $35,000 to $50,000 for his trouble and be assured of a glittering array of future sales across the years. But the Fates and the public rarely reward any writer so generously; and the beginning writer who hopes to make his fortune with a ream of paper and a few typewriter ribbons has much to learn.

We remember with sympathetic amusement a young man who, on the eve of his wedding, said that he was going to be a writer—a full-time free-lance writer—and that he had decided to write only for magazines like *The Atlantic*. He may surprise us; but we won't try to hold our breath awaiting his success.

☆ ☆ ☆

While the above discussion concerns book contracts, sales of stories to magazine editors also merit consideration. Reputable magazines usually buy only first North American serial rights. This means that the author retains the right to resell the work to foreign or foreign-language publishers, to compilers of anthologies, to television or motion-picture producers and, later on, to reprint-magazines. Often a novel will first appear in a magazine and later in a hard-cover or paperbacked book. Do not sign any contract or letter of agreement that gives the magazine publisher rights other than those of magazine publishing in the American market. And do not sell your work to a foreign publisher before it has been published in America. To do so may cost you your American copyright protection.

A writer ordinarily sells a story to a magazine, not under

any written contract, but under an oral understanding. In the case of a short story or novelette, the writer simply writes the tale and sends it to the editor, who buys or rejects it. If the magazine accepting a story is a first-class one, the writer is paid upon acceptance; if a second-class one, when the story appears in print. The terms of the purchase are often printed on the check. A photocopy of this check is a good way to record the terms. Another way is to copy the data from the check before depositing it in the bank. If the terms are unacceptable—for instance, if the publisher claims "all rights"—hold the check and voice your objections promptly. Only when you receive a modification of the terms in writing should you deposit the check at the bank.

In selling a novel, a professional writer writes only an outline and three or four chapters. When the prospective buyer is a book publisher, the editor decides from this sample whether it is suitable for his list. If the decision is favorable, he offers the writer a contract.

Contracts are not written for magazine sales. If after studying the sample, the editor thinks the story promising, he will report to the author that he expects to buy it. The writer can then complete the tale with a fair assurance that the sale has been made. There is still a chance that the rest of the story may be so poor that the editor, despite his oral commitment, will reject the work. This, however, happens very rarely.

At the present time, the pulp-paper magazines pay somewhere between 2¢ and 5¢ a word for the average story or article. Poems, if bought at all, are paid for by the line. Anthology rights may bring a flat rate payment of around $150. In some cases, the author can persuade the anthologizer to give him an additional percentage of the royalties earned by the book, although anthologies seldom sell well enough to command many sizable royalty payments beyond the advance.

If the work should come to the attention of television or motion-picture producers—and works come to their attention by way of corps of professional readers who do nothing but study books and magazines for promising material—it would be wise to hire a theatrical agent to negotiate the film or television contract, for this is a very difficult and complex market. One reputable theatrical agency is the William Morris Agency, 1350 Avenue of the Americas, New York, New York 10019.

☆ ☆ ☆

Although keeping accurate records is a bore and a chore, records are essential and should be started with the submission of your first manuscript. It is far easier to maintain good records from the start than it is to recapture unremembered facts months or years later.

Thirty-five years ago, Robert Heinlein taught the de Camps to keep the details of each piece of work on 4" x 6" or 5" x 7" cards in a small metal box. Each writing effort, whether completed or not, is given an opus number; and the card is updated each time the piece is submitted, sold, or resold. If you study the sample card with care, you will see exactly what information a writer should record.

```
THE MAGIC TURNSTILE                              Opus 39
    Short story: 3,500 words. Written 1/3/75-2/14/75.
Time taken to write: 98 hours
    Submitted:
2/18/75 to McJones at Science Stories    rejected
3/29/75 to O'Smith at Fiction Tales    rejected
5/12/75 to Ferman at The Magazine of F&SF    accepted
    Rights sold: 1st N. American Serial in English for
flat-rate payment: $105.00; paid 6/18/75. Appeared in
F&SF for 12/75.

    Anthology Rights sold: 7/7/78 to Silverberg for $100.00
non-exclusive use, with pro-rata share of additional
royalties. Appeared in his anthology THE FORTUNATE WAN-
DERER, Doubleday, 1979.

    TV Script Rights sold: 10/27/81 to Warner for $1,000;
rights revert 10/84 if not yet used.

Apply for renewal copyright in 2002 (unless law has been
changed).
```

☆ ☆ ☆

A writer also faces the problem of storing a photocopy or good carbon copy of each manuscript in such a way that he can find it easily. If the work is unfinished, unsold, or unpublished, care of the manuscript is even more essential.

The de Camps file manuscripts alphabetically in several four-drawer metal filing cabinets, the drawers of which are marked FICTION, NON-FICTION and MISCELLANEOUS. Each work, sold or unsold, is filed upright in a manila folder across the top of which appears in red crayon the title of the work and its opus number. There is, for example, in the fiction section a folder marked (THE) FALLIBLE FIEND, OPUS 586 and, farther back in the drawer, another marked LEST DARKNESS FALL, OPUS 32. This cross-reference system proves handy when you wish to look up the facts about the piece in your opus-card file box. By locating the title of the work, you quickly get its opus number. Then by flipping through the opus cards, you ascertain which rights have been sold and which are available.

When a short story or article finally appears in print, some writers cut up one or two copies of the magazine and file the printed tear sheets with the carbon copy of the original manuscript. Recently, we called Isaac Asimov long-distance to ask whether he could sell us the non-exclusive anthology rights to one of his stories. While we waited, he reached into his files, pulled out a set of tear sheets, and had them in the mail an hour later. He knew exactly where to find the story and exactly what rights were his to resell.

Once the routine has been established, these housekeeping chores are not burdensome. They become practically effortless when you realize that a professional writer is a *merchant* of tales, as well as a *creator* of tales, and that his manuscripts are his stock-in-trade. As every shopkeeper knows, it is important to keep the merchandise plainly marked and ready to hand.

Beginning writers, of course, do not need a four-drawer steel file cabinet in order to organize their manuscripts and papers. A single, drawer-sized carton will hold a number of manuscripts in an upright position in individual folders, if a book-end or small box props them up from the rear. Such a carton might also hold a group of folders containing correspondence with publishers plus a manila envelope in which to place contracts and letters of acceptance. A deep bureau drawer in the room where you type can alternatively serve as a file drawer for a number of years.

☆ ☆ ☆

Another problem in literary housekeeping must be considered. What should you do with reference notes, story outlines, false starts, first drafts, fourth drafts, and all the rest, once the finished manuscript emerges? Experienced writers cherish this "scrap paper." For one thing, it proves invaluable if a page of the finished manuscript disappears. For another, once you establish a reputation, some university will want to preserve these early drafts along with a photocopy of the finished manuscript, and a copy of the printed work, in case you prove to be a second Faulkner or in case some graduate student, yet unborn, decides to do a thesis on the way you constructed your tales.

Because present laws do not allow writers to give literary materials to universities and take a gift-tax deduction, writers send the material to the university, but do not formally give the material to it. So you collect all the scrap paper in a carton behind your writing table, organize it a bit when the job is done, and put it "on deposit" with the university that has accepted you as one of the authors whose works they are collecting. Someday, if the present Federal law is amended so that authors may donate their papers and take a tax deduction for this gift, you will present it to the library with due formality. If the law is never changed, your heirs will someday be able to give this material to the university and take a goodly gift-tax deduction for your estate.

☆ ☆ ☆

In addition to working out a system for recording the description, submissions, and sales of each literary property as well as developing a filing system for the care of each manuscript, every successful writer must organize his royalty statements. Royalty statements come in widely diverse sizes and bear information that varies from the crystal clear to the cipher cryptic.

To make matters worse, the check that accompanies most statements lures the unwary to the bank, often before he makes certain that the statement, not the check itself, bears the vital information.

Every writer must have complete records for the Internal Revenue Service about each story, poem, or novel. The records must state the gross amount paid, the date of the payment, the fees deducted by an agent, if any, and the net amount received. The Government expects taxpayers to have more detailed records every year and can call on you to show them as much as six years later.

Additional information will be necessary for the writer's protection against a careless or dishonest publisher. The writer must know whether the payment was the first or second half of a domestic advance, an advance royalty on a foreign sale, royalties earned for a given six-month period, a special book-club sale, or a flat rate (a once and only) payment. If the payment is at a flat rate—as is usually the case in sales to periodicals—does the money cover first North American serial (magazine publication) rights? Domestic and foreign rights? All rights? Non-exclusive anthology rights (one-time use in an anthology)? Or other rights?

In short, a writer's payment records must be so organized that he can tell at a glance just what and when he has been paid, and when future royalties are due. Only by studying such records can he know whether the terms of his contract are being met, whether the book or story is earning money or lying dormant, or whether he ought to approach the publisher requesting a termination of the contract.

The de Camps discovered some years ago that the opus cards in the little steel box were suitable for recording flat-rate payments on such works as short stories, poems, articles, and book reviews. But for larger works, like novels, non-fiction books, collections, and anthologies, for which payments are received over a long period of time, or for works sold at the same time to various publishers in this and other countries, much more space is required for adequate records.

We now keep a series of large loose-leaf notebooks (ours are 12" x 12" and 3½" deep) with alphabetized manila dividers, each labeled with the title of a major work. Behind each divider is a columnar accountant's sheet.

If you study the example on pages 186 and 187, you will see that after the heading, we put the name, address, and telephone number of the publisher with whom we have a current contract and the name and address of the agent, if any. Below this, we note the date of publication and summarize the major terms of the contract. Then comes a note about advance royalties paid and the periods for which royalty statements are due. Following each royalty period, we jot down the date of actual payment, the number of books sold, the gross received for the period, amounts deducted by agents, or paid to collaborators, and the net income remaining for the author.

With all this data on one page, we can readily see how the American (domestic) sales are doing and can jog the publisher if he falls behind in his royalty payments. We can tell if he has sublicensed other sales. We can see just what we received from such subsidiary sales.

Because we retain the foreign rights to most of our works, we file additional sheets behind the main contract sheet, giving similar data for each foreign publisher of that particular work. Should we ever sell television or motion picture rights, the name and address of the buyer, the terms of his contract, and a record of his payments would be entered on yet another sheet of accountant's paper.

Behind all these summary sheets, the de Camps place the publishers' half-yearly statements in reverse order—with the most recent statements on top. Since royalty statements come in a mad assortment of sizes and styles—some mere slips 3" long, others vast sheets as large as a small rug—we decided that the best way to keep the statements organized and available is to punch holes along one margin (with a dandy dime-store punch that makes three holes to match the three jaws of the ring binder) and hook the statements into the binder as soon as the information has been entered on the summary sheets.

[185]

title: LEST THE MOON FALL
publisher: Doubleday, 245 Park Ave, NY NY 10017
contact: Sharon Jarvis

Opus 40
Novel: 72,000 words
Agents: O'Jones Associates
95 13th Ave, NY NY 10103
Contact: Jan O'Jones

Contract date: March 18, 1972. Publication date: 1/9/75. Price: $10.00

Major terms: 12½ first 5,000; 15% thereafter. Statements due 9/30 and 3/30. Foreign rights retained; 1st serial rights retained; book club sales 50% to author payable on receipt; motion picture rights 75% to author. Good termination & bankruptcy clauses. PAPERBACK RIGHTS: 60% to author; Doubleday has right to make sale.

PERIOD COVERED & DATE PAID	COPIES SOLD THIS PERIOD	TO DATE	GROSS RECEIVED	AGENT'S FEE	NET RECEIVED
1st ½ of Advance 3/29/72	0	0	$1,500 00	$150 00	$1,350 00
2nd ½ of Advance 8/13/73	0	0	1,500 00	150 00	1,350 00
Total Advance	-	-	3,000 00	300 00	2,700 00
1/1/75 - 6/30/75 9/27/75	2,890	2,890	0	0	0
7/1/75 - 12/31/75 4/1/76	3,261	6,241	4,801 25	480 13	4,321 12
1/1/76 - 6/30/76 9/25/76	2,134	8,375	2,886 25	288 63	2,597 62

	Copies	Cumulative			
7/1/76 -12/31/76 3/28/77	550	8,925	825 00	82 50	742 50
BOOK CLUB SALE: 4/18/77			1,000 00	100 00	900 00
1/1/77 - 6/30/77 9/30/77	89	9,014	133 50	13 35	120 15
7/1/77 -12/31/77 3/30/78	11	9,025	16 50	1 65	14 85
On 4/15/78 sent letter to publisher asking them to republish or terminate contract.					
On 7/3/78 Paperback rights sold by Doubleday to Ballantine Books for 1979 publication. Terms: 6% for first 150,000; 8% thereafter; advance $4,000, ½ on signing, ½ on publication; 60% to author.					
1st ½ of Advance 8/19/78			1,200 00	120 00	1,080 00
2nd ½ of Advance 10/6/79			1,200 00	120 00	1,080 00

[187]

While you may choose to file your royalty statements in letter-file boxes or paper the powder room with them, the important thing to remember is that for income taxes and for checking up on publishers, you need complete, readily retrievable records of every dollar earned over many, many years.

☆ ☆ ☆

Money management for writers is not confined to knowing how to bargain before signing a contract or how to keep records for the IRS and for defense against the short-comings of publishers, important as these skills are. Free-lance writers are self-employed persons, for the most part. As self-employed persons, they not only must make special Social Security payments with their income tax, but also have to lay plans while they are young against the day when health or age makes an active writing career an impossibility.

Fortunately, in 1974 the United States Government passed an improved law covering retirement plans for the self-employed. Under the liberalized plans—often called Keogh plans—self-employed persons may put away up to 15% of their net income in a trust fund run by one of many banks or savings and loan associations. These savings earn large rates of interest and escape taxation by the Federal Government as long as the owner does not invade the principal of the fund.

At the age of 59½, the retirement fund becomes available to the saver without penalty, if he desires to draw on it. He must withdraw at least 10% a year when he reaches the age of 70½. While the money withdrawn is taxed along with the person's current income, this income is likely to be lower than it was during peak earning years. Therefore, the savings tend to be taxed at a lower rate. By saving, let us say, $1,000 a year for thirty years at current interest rates of 7½% for long term savings certificates, a writer can build a retirement fund of $120,008.24. Such a tax-sheltered way to build security at least deserves consideration.

☆ ☆ ☆

For many beginning writers, the cost of getting started presents an enormous stumbling block. It is, as we have said, best to begin a writing career as a weekend project while holding an undemanding job for bread-and-butter money. Other alternatives, however, are available to a talented new writer.

College scholarships and financial aid may be available to a would-be writer who is the child of a deceased serviceman, the offspring of a minister, a member of some minority group, or the relative of someone in a particular company, union, or fraternal organization. The list is endless; but until recent times, few people knew what scholarship money was available or how to find it. Now much of this information has been fed into a computer, which, for a fee, will provide exhaustive, individualized lists of scholarship sources. The company with this computer is Scholarship Search, 7 West 51 Street, New York, New York 10019.

Books listing sources of financial aid may also be available in your local library. One such is *Student Aid Annual,* published by Chronicle Guidance Publications, Inc., Moravia, New York 13118. Another is *Financial Aids for Higher Education,* by Oreon Keeslar, William C. Brown Company.

For the more mature writer who needs a financial boost, the Federal Government has instituted a program of National Endowment for the Arts Fellowship Grants. These grants, worth $5,000 each, are given away every two years to qualified creative writers. In 1974, one hundred fifty-four writers in 33 states received these grants. They are worth investigating.

Sometimes a beginning writer—or even an established writer—yearns for a quiet corner in which to hide until his thoughts become a story. Among the all too few people who have perceived this need and tried to meet it is a woman and her daughter who offer writers an inexpensive retreat in their country estate. If a writer is accepted, he is given a room and all his meals for a period of not less than two weeks in the beautiful Virginia countryside. For further information, write The Virginia Center for the Creative Arts, Box 3720, Charlottesville, Virginia 22903.

The writer who wishes to become thoroughly professional must by now realize that there is much to be mastered about the business side of writing. To be a success in the present-day world, it is not enough to be a brilliant spinner of tales. A thorough grounding in the ways of publishers and the public is essential. Sound knowledge of Federal and state tax laws is of the utmost importance. Time must be devoted these mundane matters if you wish to enjoy the rewards of your labors during your lifetime. It is fine to become a posthumous best seller, but it is vastly more pleasurable to become reasonably well-off and reasonably well-known while you are still alive.

AND WHEN
YOU HAVE ARRIVED . . . .

According to the Census of 1970, there are in all the United States somewhat over 26,300 authors. Of these, 7,691 are women and 18,685 are men. These figures include staff writers on periodicals, persons who write part time, and hopefuls who list themselves as authors long before they have had a significant number of published works.

Only 150 to 250 American authors are writers of imaginative fiction—people whose names appear on published stories in the genre at least once or twice a year. Of these, in turn, only a fraction actually support themselves and their families solely on the proceeds of imaginative writing.

There are no reliable figures on the earnings of full-time, free-lance writers of imaginative fiction. It is evident that their earnings vary widely. If one can judge from their wordage and present-day rates of payment, the leaders in the field make a comfortable living. Still, it is a rare writer of science fiction or fantasy whose average income is larger than that of a well-paid schoolteacher.

The profession, moreover, gives no security whatsoever. The writer can never coast. No matter how successful he becomes, he can never assume that henceforth everything will be easy. If you want to ride the coattails of success, you have to go on doing research, observing people, polishing your technique, and ransacking your unconscious for new ideas. Unless you do, you will soon be elbowed aside by others with brighter, newer ideas and approaches to the art of writing that you have never dreamed of. Someone justly said: writing is the only profession that becomes harder the longer you practice it.

Lest these facts dampen your enthusiasm, let us hasten to add that writing for a living has intangible advantages far greater than the ability to work sitting down. A writer is his own boss. He meets interesting people. He can travel and charge off the costs as business expense by following each trip with salable articles or stories to prove to the Internal Revenue Service that the travel was for business, not only for pleasure.

The writer who works at home enjoys some small economic advantage over the average businessman or businesswoman. There is no commuter fare to pay. Old clothes can be worn. Lunches are inexpensive, homemade snacks. The writing room is tax-deductible. Time can be adapted to other obligations.

Free-lance writers also have glamour in the eyes of the public. They enjoy occasional ego-lifts from seeing their names in print, in even so humble a place as a home-town newspaper. And everyone knows about the poor devil who struggled along for twenty years and then hit the jackpot— had his book selected by a big book club, or won a cash prize, or sold a story to the movies. Such success stories, while rare in real life, stimulate a lot of people to dream the great American dream of sudden success.

☆ ☆ ☆

To be a good writer, you must be a part of your community. Like every successful human being, you have to participate in the activities of those around you. You can put your skills to work as an advisor to a local library or a lecturer at an adult evening school. You can interest school children in imaginative fiction by reading aloud some of the greatest stories or talking about the field. You can do any one of hundreds of community tasks where an articulate person can give focus to community needs.

Interacting with your neighbors is also good for business. In today's world, a writer has to do a considerable job of self-promotion. Where better to start than by letting those among whom you live get to know your name through meetings and the local press?

Once established as a local author, you have a springboard to wider publicity and somewhat more experience in presenting to the world the personna you wish to project. Everybody has to develop the sort of mantle he wishes to wear throughout his life. The eccentric pose has been killed by a generation of young people who have vied for eccentricity. The matinee idol or temperamental motion-picture star went out of style forty years ago. So be yourself. Be pleasant; be friendly; be moderately unassuming but aware of your own worth—that is Asimov's way, and a better way to be could not be found. He has integrity and thousands of friends.

At the same time, no writer can give all his time to his public. As soon as a writer becomes known and liked, he finds himself surrounded by admirers. Philip Wylie, in the May 1950 *Atlantic Monthly,* complained bitterly of the way admirers telephoned him at all hours, wrote long letters and expected longer replies, and sent innumerable books to be autographed and returned—often without adequate wrapping materials and postage. They asked for free criticism of their manuscripts and peered through his windows to see what a "real author" looked like.

There are ways to cope with the too-pervasive overtures of fans and friends. Let it be known that you cannot receive unannounced callers because time is the only money-making asset you have and you must not squander it. Charge for criticizing manuscripts. Answer letters with a cheery post card instead of indulging in long arguments or expositions. Lovecraft, you remember, wrote 100,000 letters and had scant time for his own creative work.

When fan groups plan a convention in your area, however, take the time to meet your admirers. Talk about professional matters all night over a few mugs of beer. Give advice; ride your hobbies; listen to comments on your work with an open ear and mind. Your admirers may teach you as much as you teach them. Do contribute to the fan magazines—not salable stories, of course, because to do so would mean the loss of income and probable loss of copyright. But let your admirers know that you admire them, too.

Never waste time writing unfriendly critics or book reviewers to justify your work. It does no good and makes you look touchy and ridiculous. You neither persuade the reviewer (who is often writing for a nation-wide syndicated review organ) nor increase your sales. If the reviewer has sound criticisms, try to profit from them. If not, forget them. There is only one exception to this rule: when a reviewer has made a gross misstatement of fact, you are justified in writing him somewhat like this: "Mr. Bunthorne appears to be misinformed. I am Isaac Bradlein, the writer, not Arnold Bradlein, the bank robber."

One other suggestion is in order here. If a writer lives in New York where many fellow-writers live, or in a writer's colony such as Taos or Carmel or the eastern tip of Cape Cod, he is often tempted to sit up all night discussing what he is going to write. Some writers find it dangerous to discuss stories which are not yet written—not because some eaves-dropper will steal their ideas, but because talking about the plot unwinds their mainspring and weakens the impulse to write the piece.

☆ ☆ ☆

A writer must give thought to his relations with his spouse and family. In order to do creative work—whether painting, acting, dancing, scientific research, or writing—a person needs solitude and peace of mind. From time immemorial, all creative workers have dreamed of an ivory tower with a good view, an automatic coffee-maker, and a dragon to guard the door. Unfortunately, the days of dragons are past.

To achieve this necessary withdrawal from humanity, authors have tried many schemes. Some write late at night when the house is quiet. This can be hard on the health if other jobs or active family members demand an early morning start. Some writers solve this problem by taking a long nap while the children are at school or their mates are away.

Well-off writers sometimes rent a small apartment for an office and keep business hours. This gives privacy but can be hard on the writer's family if the Muse beckons days and evenings, too. If a writer has a spouse and children, time must be allotted to playing with the young, acting as tutor, dating the spouse, or working as a gardener, plumber, or handyman. Women writers often have the added burden of being a homemaker, child tender, and family chauffeur.

Unless these matters can be worked out in a rational way, there is grave danger that a devoted, dedicated writer may find himself without a family. More marriages have foundered because of a demanding Muse than because of a human rival. Wives of writers, more than husbands, are liable to find themselves excluded from the intense, ivory-towered existence demanded of any disciple of the arts. Wives, more than husbands, are likely to find marriage to a full-time or an active part-time writer intolerable.

Even for this serious problem, there are solutions. For one thing, the writer can see to it that time is set aside periodically to socialize with his spouse's friends. If the prospect seems pallid beside the joy of hovering over a typewriter, hide the fact; stifle the yawns. Anyone who acts as a guardian at the door of the ivory tower deserves an occasional evening out and some time alone with the great mind. Besides, writers can use these evenings to observe the way ordinary people talk, think, and act. This is the stuff of which the next story is made. For these evenings, writers can surrender the center of the stage and do all they can to make their mates feel important, attended, and beloved.

There is another, even more desirable, solution to the problem of an author's need for privacy, care, and attention, and the spouse's equally important need for acclaim and a sense of self-worth. The problem can be solved by forming a literary partnership with the spouse. If the non-writing partner is willing to learn the business side of writing and becomes a business manager, the writer is spared many tedious hours of bookkeeping, tax work, and business-letter writing, to say nothing about sessions with stock brokers, bankers, and insurance salesmen.

Not all writers' partners have the training to do these many complex operations; but, assuming they are persons of reasonable intelligence, all of them can learn.

There are immense benefits to be gained from this division of labor. The writer's spouse learns the special problems of the business that puts the food on the table. Knowing how to read a contract to catch unfavorable terms, how to record royalties, and how to keep tax records can increase the writer's income significantly. Best of all, being a partner with the writer gives the spouse a warm interest in the success of the venture and a real sense of contributing to it. Spouses who know nothing about the writing business often feel unwanted and unloved when, after spending years protecting the writer from the strains of daily life, they must stand aside and watch the great author bask in the glow of public admiration. Business partners, on the other hand, can munch the sandwiches at the author's tea and tally up the extra dollars that are bound to follow the lecture, television appearance, or autograph party.

The junior author of this book learned many years ago that a partnership was the only way for a writer's spouse to be happily married. In the de Camp family, indeed, the partnership has been extended to collaborations on a number of books as well as on business management. While this particular solution is not possible for every couple with an author in the family, it is the ultimate way for a writer to achieve family harmony and good-will. In some circles, Sprague is the honored guest; in others, Catherine receives the kudos for her own books; in still others, we share the honors jointly. And all the time we tend the business to protect the family literary works and to exploit them efficiently.

Moreover, if an author and his spouse are partners and if the writing partner dies, there need be no worry about the proper handling of the writer's literary estate. On-the-job training about such matters as agents, contract terms, copyrights, tax deductions, the location and availability of the various literary works—these and other matters of importance to professional free-lance writers will prove invaluable to the author's widow, widower, or heirs. A lack of such training cost the heirs of Edgar Rice Burroughs a fortune because they failed to renew copyrights on some of the Tarzan stories. Books that once sold for a few hundred dollars may, years later, become paperback best-sellers, foreign language hardbacks, or television plays and net a neat piece of change to those who own and properly manage the rights.

☆ ☆ ☆

We have explored a writer's relation to his community and to his family. What is a writer's obligation to himself? We believe that a writer should use his skills to promote the welfare and happiness of his readers, not to exploit his fellow humans to make a fast buck. It is dishonest to write trash when you can write a worthwhile story. It is dishonest to state as fact that little green men from Mars built the Pyramids or that charms can guarantee anyone health, wealth, and happiness.

In a science-fiction story, it is quite all right to have Martians visit Earth. In a fantasy tale, magic is bound to work. But every reader of imaginative fiction knows that he is reading fairy tales—fairy tales, perhaps, that contain a dash of prediction, a kernel of truth.

Science fiction is a heady mix of the world's traditional myths, modern scientific knowledge, and men's dreams of a better world in years to come. Science fiction should offer its readers an insight into the probable world of tomorrow. It should take the evidence culled from recent scientific research and leap to conclusions that may or may not be proven correct ten or a hundred years hence. It should point out the dangers of atomic warfare, of a deteriorating gene pool, of an overly-complex social organization, of over-populating this small globe of ours.

Science fiction—and fantasy, too—should stimulate the reader's curiosity and start his brain cells quivering. It should be well-written and well-punctuated, lest the printed words interfere with the ideas they carry. Most of all, imaginative fiction should be a window through which the reader can view the wonders of the world of today, the glories of the past, and the promise of the future.

SCIENCE FICTION HANDBOOK, REVISED

THE WORLD OF IMAGINATIVE FICTION

1. Marjorie Nicholson: *Voyages to the Moon* (New York: Macmillan, 1948), pp. 1f; phonograph record of the broadcast published by Longines–Witnauer Co.

2. *Time,* July 10, 1939, p. 32.

3. "Doom Beyond Jupiter," in *Harper's Magazine,* September 1939, pp. 445-48.

4. *Astounding Science Fiction,* June 1949, pp. 158-61.

MODERN IMAGINATIVE FICTION

1. Burroughs had sent in the manuscript under the name of "Normal Bean" (Burroughs's little joke) but the typesetter erred.

2. Eleven, if one counts *John Carter of Mars,* a paperback (New York: Ballantine Books, 1965) comprising two novelettes about John Carter.

3. "Venerian" is the right adjective derived from "Venus," whose Latin genetive is *Veneris.* The term "Venusian," often heard, properly refers to an inhabitant of the ancient Italian city of Venusia.

4. Pronounced LAY-vun-hook.

5. Accent on the penult; rhymes with "rainy."

6. H. P. Lovecraft: *The Outsider and Others,* (Sauk City,

WI: Arkham House, 1939), p. 549.

7. Lord Dunsany: *The Book of Wonder* (Boston: Luce, 1912), pp. 74, 117.

8. "Binder" rhymes with "cinder"; "Eando" stands for "E. and O." because Otto Binder began writing in collaboration with his brother Earl.

9. For the dramatic story of Hubbard's adventures, see George Malko: *Scientology, the Now Religion* (1970); Daniel Cohen: *Masters of the Occult* (1971); Robert Kaufman: *Inside Scientology* (1972); and Christopher Evans: *Cults of Unreason* (1973).

EDITORS AND PUBLISHERS

1. James Boswell: *Life of Dr. Johnson,* II, p. 16.

2. *The Lord of the Rings,* not counting the lengthy appendices, comes to about 600,000 words.

3. Bug-eyed monsters.

4. *Startling Stories,* October 1952, pp. 6, 128; slightly condensed.

5. "The Science of Science Fiction Writing," in *Of Worlds Beyond* ed. L. A. Eshbach (Reading PA: Fantasy Press, 1947), p. 96.

READERS AND WRITERS

1. *Astounding Science Fiction,* July 1949, pp. 161f.

PREPARING FOR A SCIENCE-FICTION CAREER

1. M. P. Shiel: *The Purple Cloud* (New York: Vanguard, 1930), p. vii. A last-man-on-earth story originally published in the U.K. in 1901.

2. The first sentence uses "like" for "as"; the second, "providing" for "provided."

THOSE CRAZY IDEAS

1. Charles S. Ingerman of the *Ladies Home Journal,* in a

speech at the Philadelphia Regional Writers' Conference, June 20, 1951.

2. Esbach: *Of Worlds Beyond*, p. 26

3. Bernard De Voto: "The Easy Chair," in *Harper's Magazine*, November 1952.

PLOTTING AN IMAGINATIVE STORY

1. "The Siren Song of Academe," in *Galaxy Science Fiction Magazine*, March 1975, pp. 73f.

2. Preface to *Seven Famous Novels by H. G. Wells* (New York: Knopf, 1934), p. viii.

3. Katherine MacLean, "The Snowball Effect," *Galaxy Science Fiction*, September 1952.

4. Introduction to *World of Wonder* (New York: Twayne, 1951), p. 21.

5. Also published as *Cosmic Manhunt* (USA) and *A Planet Called Kirshna* (UK).

6. Eshbach: *Of Worlds Beyond*, pp. 50ff.

7. *Strange and Fantastic Stories* (Whittlesey House, 1946). Mountdrago is possibly modeled upon the real Lord Curzon (1859-1925).

8. Eshbach: *Of Worlds Beyond*, pp. 12ff.

9. *Fantasy & Science Fiction*, June 1952, p. 18.

WRITING AN IMAGINATIVE STORY

1. Isaac Asimov: *Pebble in the Sky* (Garden City, N.Y.: Doubleday, 1950), p. 9.

2. De Camp: "The Hand of Zei," *Astounding Science Fiction*, Oct. 1950, p. 7.

3. Thorne Smith: *Skin and Bones* (Doubleday Doran, 1933), p. 1.

4. Robert A. Heinlein: "Blowups Happen," in *The Man Who Sold the Moon* (Chicago: Shasta, 1950), p. 105.

5. De Camp: *Divide and Rule* (Reading PA: Fantasy Press, 1948), p. 9.

6. De Camp: "The Saxon Pretender," in *Sprague de Camp's New Anthology* (London: Hamilton, 1954), p. 99.

7. Alexander M. Phillips: *The Mislaid Charm* (Philadelphia: Prime Press, 1947), p. 38.

8. De Camp & Fletcher Pratt: "The Ancestral Amethyst," *Fantasy & Science Fiction,* August 1952, p. 17.

9. Thorne Smith: *The Thorne Smith Triplets* (Sun Dial, 1944), p. 14.

10. De Camp: *The Glory That Was* (New York: Avalon, 1960), pp. 38f.

11. *Ibid.,* p. 83.

SELLING AN IMAGINATIVE STORY

1. Eshbach: *Of Worlds Beyond,* p. 17.

BIBLIOGRAPHY

I. SCIENCE-FICTION NOVELS
AND SINGLE-AUTHOR COLLECTIONS.

This reading list is for those of you new to science fiction and fantasy and for teachers planning courses in the field. It is largely based on surveys taken of readers' preferences in 1953 by P. Schuyler Miller and in 1975 by Charles and Dena Brown, and on a survey of reading lists for science-fiction courses which was made in 1975 by Jack Williamson. Most of these books are available in paperback editions, reprinted from time to time; and they may be obtained from the various bookstores which specialize in the field and whose advertisements may be found in science-fiction and fantasy magazines.

Anderson, Poul: *The High Crusade.*

Asimov, Isaac: *Foundation* (the 24th World Science Fiction Convention voted this and its sequels to be the best all-time series of novels).

————: *I, Robot* (collection of stories about robots).

Bester, Alfred: *The Stars My Destination.*

Bradbury, Ray: *The Martian Chronicles* (a collection of stories).

Brunner, John: *Stand on Zanzibar* (population problems in the near future).

Burroughs, Edgar Rice: *A Princess of Mars* (the archetypical action story).

Campbell, John W. Jr.: *Who Goes There?* (a collection that includes the story of the same name).

Clarke, Arthur C.: *Childhood's End.*

Clement, Hal: *Mission of Gravity.*

de Camp, L. Sprague: *Lest Darkness Fall.*

del Rey, Lester: *. . . and Some Were Human* (collection).

Heinlein, Robert A.: *The Green Hills of Earth* (a collection that includes the story of the same name; short stories of Heinlein's "Future History" series).

————: *The Moon Is a Harsh Mistress.*

————: *Stranger in a Strange Land* (this book enjoyed remarkable popularity outside the field in recent years).

Herbert, Frank: *Dune* (another example of a work which became widely known outside of the usual science-fiction readers; it was the all-time most popular science-fiction novel in the 1975 survey).

Huxley, Aldous: *Brave New World.*

Le Guin, Ursula K.: *The Left Hand of Darkness.*

Leiber, Fritz: *Gather, Darkness!.*

Miller, Walter M.: *A Canticle for Leibowitz.*

Niven, Larry: *Ringworld* (adventure with a strong scientific background).

Orwell, George: *Nineteen Eighty-Four* (the classic negative utopia).

Pohl, Frederik, & Kornbluth, C. M.: *The Space Merchants* (advertising and big business in the future).

Stapledon, W. Olaf: *Last and First Men.*

Sturgeon, Theodore: *More Than Human.*

van Vogt, A. E.: *Slan* (this was the all-time most popular novel in the 1953 survey).

Wells, H. G.: *The Time Machine* (a collection that includes the famous classic story of the same name).

Zelazny, Roger: *Lord of Light.*

II. SCIENCE-FICTION ANTHOLOGIES.

These books contain many of the most popular shorter works in the field. They are listed in order of publication:

Healy, Raymond J., & McComas, J. Francis (eds.): *Adventures in Time and Space,* also published as *Famous Science*

Fiction Stories (published in 1946; the most popular book in the 1953 survey, and one of the very few anthologies that has remained in print almost continuously; a sampling of early, readable science fiction).

Conklin, Groff (ed.): *The Best of Science Fiction* (another popular, 1946 collection of early science fiction).

Silverberg, Robert (ed.): *The Science Fiction Hall of Fame, Volume I* (this collection, published in 1970, is based on a survey of the members of the Science Fiction Writers of America; it is limited to works less than 15,000 words long).

Bova, Ben (ed.): *The Science Fiction Hall of Fame, Volumes II-A & II-B* (published in 1973, this collection of stories between 15,000 words long and novel-length was selected in the same way as *Volume I,* above).

III. FANTASY NOVELS
AND SINGLE-AUTHOR COLLECTIONS.

The following list, for those who would like to familiarize themselves with this field, is our own selection.

Anderson, Poul: *The Broken Sword.*

Cabell, James Branch: *Figures of Earth* (first of a series).

Collier, John: *Fancies and Goodnights* (collection).

Dunsany, Lord: *Gods, Men and Ghosts* (one of several collections).

Eddison, Eric R.: *The Worm Ouroboros.*

Finney, Charles: *The Circus of Dr. Lao.*

Howard, Robert E.; de Camp, L. Sprague; Carter, Lin; & Nyberg, Björn: *Conan* (archetypical swordplay and sorcery, one of a series).

Le Guin, Ursula K.: *A Wizard of Earthsea* (first of a series).

Leiber, Fritz: *Swords in the Mist* (one of a series).

Lewis, C. S.: *That Hideous Strength.*

Lovecraft, H. P.: *The Dunwich Horror* (one of several collections).

Machen, Arthur: *The Three Imposters.*

Merritt, A.: *The Ship of Ishtar.*

Norton, Andre: *Witch World* (first of a series).

Pratt, Fletcher, & de Camp, L. Sprague: *The Incomplete*

Enchanter (first of a series).

Smith, Clark Ashton: *Zothique* (one of several collections).

Smith, Thorne: *Night Life of the Gods.*

Stoker, Bram: *Dracula.*

Tolkien, J. R. R.: *The Lord of the Rings* (the famous three-volume fantasy novel).

Vance, Jack: *The Dying Earth* (collection with a common setting).

White, T. H.: *The Once and Future King* (the book on which *Camelot* was based).

Williamson, Jack: *Darker Than You Think.*

IV. BIBLIOGRAPHIES
OF FANTASY AND SCIENCE FICTION.

These are useful when you wish to locate some specific work among back-issue magazines or anthologies, and especially should you edit an anthology yourself.

Bleiler, Everett F.: *The Checklist of Fantastic Literature.* Chicago: Shasta Publishers, 1948; West Linn OR: FAX, 1972 (lists over 5,000 books in the field).

Briney, Robert, & Wood, Edward: *SF Bibliographies.* Chicago: Advent:Publishers, 1972, revised edition forthcoming (a bibliography of bibliographies).

Burger, Joanne: *The Checklist of Paperback Literature.* West Linn OR: FAX, forthcoming (extends Bleiler, above, to paperbacks).

Cole, Walter R.: *A Checklist of Science-Fiction Anthologies.* Author, 1964; New York: Arno Press, 1975.

Day, Donald B.: *Index to the Science-Fiction Magazines 1926-1950.* Portland OR: Perri Press, 1952.

Metcalf, Norman: *The Index of Science Fiction Magazines 1951-1965.* Available directly from the publisher, J. Ben Stark, 113 Ardmore Rd., Berkeley CA 94707, 1968.

New England Science Fiction Association: *Index to the Science Fiction Magazines [dates]* (title varies). Available directly from the publisher at Box G, M.I.T. Branch, Cambridge MA 02139 (a continuing series of bibliographies, covering the period from 1951 up to the present).

Tymn, Marshall: *The Checklist of Fantastic Literature II.*

West Linn OR: FAX, forthcoming (extends Bleiler, above, from 1947 up to 1974).

V. NON-FICTION WORKS
ABOUT FANTASY AND SCIENCE FICTION.

This list covers histories of the field, biographies of authors, criticism, books on writing imaginative fiction, and related subjects.

Atheling, William, Jr. (pseud. of James Blish): *The Issue at Hand* and *More Issues at Hand.* Chicago: Advent: Publishers, 1964 & 1970 (criticism).

Bailey, J. O.: *Pilgrims Through Space and Time: Trends and Patterns in Scientific and Utopian Fiction.* New York: Argus Books, 1947; Westport CT: Greenwood Press, 1972 (the pioneering work on the origins and early development of science fiction).

Bova, Ben: *Notes to a Science Fiction Writer.* New York: Charles Scribners' Sons, forthcoming (a book on writing SF by a leading SF editor).

Bretnor, Reginald (ed.): *Modern Science Fiction, Its Meaning and Its Future.* New York: Coward-McCann, 1953; Westport CT: Greenwood Press, forthcoming (essays by leading SF writers on the field).

———— (ed.): *Science Fiction Today and Tomorrow: a Discursive Symposium.* New York: Harper and Row, 1974.

———— (ed.): *The Craft of Science Fiction and Science Fantasy.* New York: Harper and Row, forthcoming.

Davenport, Basil (ed.): *The Science Fiction Novel.* Chicago: Advent:Publishers, 1959.

Eshbach, Lloyd A. (ed.): *Of Worlds Beyond: the Science of Science Fiction.* Reading PA: Fantasy Press, 1947; Chicago: Advent:Publishers, 1964 (essays on writing SF by Campbell, de Camp, Heinlein, E. E. Smith, Taine, van Vogt, & Williamson).

Knight, Damon: *In Search of Wonder.* Chicago: Advent: Publishers, 1956, 2nd edition, 1967 (criticism).

Koontz, Dean: *Writing Popular Fiction.* Cincinnati: Writer's Digest, 1972 (devoted in part to SF).

Lovecraft, H. P.: *Supernatural Horror in Literature.* New

York: Abramson, 1945; New York: Dover Publications, 1973 (paper).

Moskowitz, Sam: *Explorers of the Infinite: Shapers of Science Fiction.* New York: World Publishing Co., 1963; Westport CT: Hyperion Press, 1974 (biographies of SF writers).

————: *Seekers of Tomorrow: Masters of Modern Science Fiction.* New York: World Publishing Co., 1966; Westport CT: Hyperion Press, 1974 (biographies of SF writers).

Rogers, Alva: *A Requiem for Astounding.* Chicago: Advent: Publishers, 1964 (a history of *Astounding Science Fiction* magazine).

Tuck, Donald H.: *The Encyclopedia of Science Fiction and Fantasy.* Chicago: Advent:Publishers; Volume A-L, 1974; balance forthcoming (a monumental survey of the field: biographical data, anthology contents, and so on; a valuable reference work).

Warner, Harry, Jr.: *All Our Yesterdays: an Informal History of Science Fiction Fandom in the Forties.* Chicago: Advent:Publishers, 1969.

Weinberg, Robert: *The Weird Tales Story.* West Linn OR: FAX, forthcoming (a history of *Weird Tales* magazine).

Wertham, Frederic: *The World of Fanzines: a Special Form of Communication.* Carbondale IL: Southern Illinois University Press, 1973.

Williamson, Jack: *Teaching SF.* Available directly from the author at Box 761, Portales NM 88130, 1975.

———— (ed.): *Science Fiction: Education for Tomorrow.* Baltimore: Mirage Press, forthcoming (a collection of essays on teaching SF).

VI. REFERENCE WORKS
IN SCIENCE, HISTORY, AND TECHNOLOGY.

The following, based on recommendations by some of our colleagues, is a sample of the wide reading in technical fields required of a successful science-fiction writer.

Asimov, Isaac: *Asimov's Guide to Science.* New York: Basic Books, 1972.

————: *The Dark Ages.* Boston: Houghton-Mifflin Co., 1968

(a broad, basic overview of the period).

Baez, Albert V.: *The New College Physics: a Spiral Approach.* San Francisco: W. H. Freeman & Co., 1967.

Bracewell, Ronald N.: *The Galactic Club: Intelligent Life in Outer Space.* San Francisco: W. H. Freeman & Co., 1975 (a recent review of scientific speculation in this field).

Colbert, Edwin H.: *Evolution of the Vertebrates,* 2nd edition. New York: John Wiley & Sons, 1969 (paleontology).

Cottrell, Leonard: *Concise Encyclopedia of Archaeology.* New York: Hawthorn, 1971 (overview of the subject on a basic level).

Dole, S. H.: *Habitable Planets for Man,* 2nd edition. New York: American Elsevier, 1970.

Hall, Edward T.: *The Silent Language.* Garden City NY: Doubleday, 1959 (cloth); 1973 (paper) (anthropology and non-verbal communication).

Holvey, David N. (ed.): *The Merck Manual of Diagnosis and Therapy.* Rahway NJ: Merck & Co., 1972 (a compact and well-organized discussion of everything that can go wrong with the human organism, including symptoms and treatments; unless your characters suffer nothing worse than sniffles, this is very handy).

Johnson, Daniel (ed.): *Village Technology Handbook.* Available directly from the publisher, V.I.T.A., 3706 Rhode Island Ave., Mt Ranier MD 20822, 1975 (this and the earlier *Remote Areas Development Manual,* published by Community Development Counselling Service, 1515 North Court House Rd., Arlington VA 22201, are guidebooks for those who make a specific effort to improve conditions in underdeveloped, remote areas with local resources or minimal outside assistance, covering practical shoestring technology with lots of hints on what can go wrong; with some extrapolation, either is an excellent reference on colonizing a remote, earth-like planet).

Kinder, H., & Hilgemann, W.: *The Anchor Atlas of World History, from the Stone Age to the Eve of the French Revolution.* Garden City NY: Anchor/Doubleday, 1974 (paper) (a set of maps with chronological outlines of history on facing pages; a concise and comprehensive outline of history, with a second volume forthcoming).

Kline, Morris: *Mathematics and the Physical World.* New York: T. Y. Crowell, 1959 (cloth); New York: Apollo Editions, 1969 (paper).

Kroeber, A. L.: *Anthropology: Race, Language, Culture, Psychology, Prehistory.* New York: Harcourt Brace Jovanovich, 1948.

Larousse Encyclopedia of the Earth. New York: Crown, 1972.

Moore, Patrick: *The Concise Atlas of the Universe.* Chicago: Rand, McNally, 1975 (an abridged and updated edition of *The Atlas of the Universe*).

Nesbitt, Pond, & Allen: *The Survival Book.* New York: Funk & Wagnalls, 1968 (paper) (an excellent source of information on the hazards of being stranded on hostile terrain and on what your characters can do to cope with materials likely to be on hand).

Oparin, A. I.: *Life: Its Nature, Origin, and Development.* London: Oliver & Boyd, 1961 (a discussion on how life might have formed on earth and on other planets by natural chemical processes).

Sagan, Carl, & Shklovsky, I. S.: *Intelligent Life in the Universe.* San Francisco: Holden-Day, 1966 (cloth); New York: Dell, 1968 (paper) (this dialogue gathers together considerable detail on all branches of science that bear on intelligent life).

Stone, George Cameron: *A Glossary of the Construction, Decoration and Use of Arms and Armor.* New York: Jack Brussel, originally printed in 1934 and recently reprinted (the definitive work on the subject).

Tannahill, Reay: *Food in History.* New York: Stein & Day, 1973 (cloth); 1974 (paper).

Weast, Robert C. (ed.): *The Handbook of Chemistry and Physics.* Cleveland: CRC Press, 1971 (this is the well-known "Rubber Handbook"; a valuable compendium of physical and chemical characteristics, etc.).

VII. MYTHOLOGY AND LEGENDS.

A comprehensive knowledge of the myths and legends of past and present cultures is essential not only for the fantasy writer but also for the writer of science fiction.

Barber, Richard: *King Arthur in Legend and History.* Totowa NJ: Rowman & Littlefield, 1973.

Bulfinch, Thomas: *The Age of Chivalry and Legends.* New York: New American Library, 1962 (paper, reprint of the 1863 edition).

Byfield, Barbara Ninde: *The Book of Weird.* Garden City NY: Doubleday, 1973 (paper) (original hardcover titled *The Glass Harmonica;* a basic guide to the terms used in fairy-tales).

Fort, Charles: *The Books of Charles Fort.* New York: Dover Publications, 1973 (paper reprint of the 1941 edition) (a source-book for a modern mythology).

Graves, Robert: *The Greek Myths.* New York: Braziller, 1959.

Grimal, Pierre (ed.): *Larousse World Mythology.* New York: Putnam, 1968.

Homer: *The Iliad* and *The Odyssey,* various editions.

Lang, Andrew (ed.): *The Red Fairy Book.* New York: Dover Publications, 1966 (paper, reprint of the 1890 edition).

———— (ed.): *The Arabian Nights Entertainments.* New York: Dover Publications, 1969 (paper, reprint of the 1898 edition).

Malory, Sir Thomas: *Le Mort d'Arthur,* various editions.

Morris, William (translator): *Volsunga Saga: the Story of the Volsungs and Niblungs.* New York: Collier Books, 1962 (paper, reprint).

Thompson, Stith: *The Folktale.* New York: Holt, Rinehart & Winston, 1951.

Young, Jean I. (translator): *The Prose Edda of Snorri Sturlson: Tales from Norse Mythology.* Berkeley CA: The University of California Press, 1973.

VIII. BASIC REFERENCES FOR WRITERS.

These are references which you will need to consult with

some regularity; they deal with words, style, grammar, and the like.

Dougherty, Fitzgerald, & Bolander: *Instant Spelling Dictionary*. Available directly from the publisher, Career Institute, 555 East Lange St., Mundelein IL 60060, 1967 (a dictionary big enough to list all the obscure words and definitions will be unhandy when all you need is the spelling of a fairly common word; instead of trying to make one book serve both purposes, get a full-sized dictionary for the definitions and a spelling dictionary, such as this one).

Little, Fowler, & Coulson: *The Shorter Oxford Dictionary on Historical Principles*. Oxford & New York: Oxford University Press, 1973 (although this is an abridgement of the monumental, 13-volume *Oxford English Dictionary,* it is still larger than most "unabridged" dictionaries).

Strunk, William, Jr.: *Elements of Style,* 2nd edition, revised by E. B. White. New York: Macmillan, 1972 (concise, clear, and authoritative).

Roget's International Thesaurus, 3rd edition. New York: T. Y. Crowell, 1962 (useful for giving you a selection of words from which you can choose the one that precisely fits your meaning; avoid the temptation to use it to find a long word when a shorter will do or to find synonyms for "he said").

Bartlett, John: *Familiar Quotations,* 14th edition. Boston: Little, Brown & Co., 1968 (a storehouse of story ideas and titles; *The Oxford Dictionary of Quotations* is a similar work).

Columbia Encyclopedia. New York: Columbia University Press, 4th edition in press (an excellent one-volume work).

The Encyclopaedia Britannica, various editions (since one doesn't consult an encyclopedia for recent developments in a rapidly developing field, there is no reason you should get the latest edition; and earlier editions can be obtained quite reasonably at second-hand bookstores: the Eleventh Edition (1910-1911) is celebrated for the quality of its literary and historical articles).

INDEX

[213]